What if Canada Became the 51st State?
Food for thought!
The History, Potential Implications and Possibilities of a Borderless Future

Jessie Hionis

DEDICATION

I would like to extend a special thanks to President Donald Trump, whose wise ambition and desire for a united North America inspired me to inquire about, research and write this book about Canada becoming the 51st state. This title and its topic have not been met with little adversity. Nonetheless, the idea of a borderless future has reignited my passion for politics and international affairs and has delightfully filled my surroundings with enriching discussions about a new era for North America.

Table of Contents

Preface

The notion of Canada becoming the 51st state of the United States is one of those ideas that occasionally flares up in political discourse, media speculation, and even popular culture. While the prospect may seem implausible or even fantastical to many, it touches on deep historical ties, geopolitical considerations, and shared cultural dynamics between the two nations. With active research using various legal, academic, and online resources and AI tools such as Chat GPT and NinjaTech AI, this book aims to shed a light on the history behind the idea of merging North America. The following chapters will attempt to demystify the complexity of such an ambitious union. The potential implications and possibilities of a borderless future with Canada becoming the 51st state is vast and elaborate. This book will aim to explore the roots and ramifications of such an idea through the lenses of history, law, international relations, and public opinion.

The concept has existed on the periphery of North American politics for over a century, fueled by historical events such as War Plan Red, a 1930s U.S. military strategy for invading Canada in the event of conflict with the British Empire and punctuated by periodic comments from politicians and public figures. It has resurfaced in the modern era, most notably in the context of political banter or as a reaction to global shifts in power dynamics. Although often dismissed as an improbable or even absurd notion, its persistent reemergence and invites serious reflection on the ties that bind Canada and the United States.

This book seeks to evaluate the concept of a Canadian American union with a balanced perspective. By examining historical documents, contemporary treaties, economic relationships, and cultural exchanges, we will delve into both the advantages and proponents. The argument that a union could bolster economic stability, strengthen defense capabilities, and foster deeper collaboration in areas like environmental policy and technological innovation will also be explored. We will also look at the challenges posed by differences in governance, cultural identity, and the deeply rooted sense of sovereignty that defines both nations.

We will begin by tracing the historical origins of the idea, from the secretive War Plan Red to the 19th-century annexation debates. Moving into the present, we will consider treaties like

NAFTA and its successor, USMCA, which demonstrate both the benefits and limits of economic integration. Legal frameworks, such as Article II, Section 2 of the U.S. Constitution offer insights into how such a dramatic geopolitical shift might unfold procedurally. Through it all, we will incorporate voices from both sides of the border, including politicians, scholars, journalists, and everyday citizens, to provide a comprehensive understanding of how this concept is perceived and could be debated.

As you journey through these pages, my hope is not to advocate for or against the idea of Canada becoming the 51st state, but rather to provoke thought about the interplay between sovereignty and collaboration in an increasingly interconnected world. In doing so, this book aims to shed light on the historical roots and contemporary relevance of an enduring, and possibly improbable, topic. Whether you approach this subject with curiosity, skepticism, or fascination, I will invite you to explore the intricate layers of history, law, and identity that make this discussion so compelling.

While the discussions outlined in this book are speculative, they could provide an idea and a possible framework for understanding the monumental scope of such a grand transformation for North America.

Chapter 1
Food for Thought
The Unlikely but Thought-Provoking Possibility of Canada Becoming the 51st State

In the vast landscape of political speculation, few scenarios evoke as much intrigue, curiosity, and skepticism as the possibility of Canada becoming the 51st state of the United States. The very idea seems improbable and almost absurd, yet it raises profound questions about identity, nationalism, and the ways in which countries define themselves. At first glance, it may appear to be a fantasy, a far-fetched thought experiment with no real bearing on the present. However, if we peel back the layers of both Canadian and American public opinion, we begin to uncover a nuanced landscape of ego, knowledge, openness, and the willingness of both nations to reconsider the foundations of their national identity.

The Canadian Ego: A Reluctant Neighbor

Canada's identity is often framed as one of quiet distinction and independence. Canadians pride themselves on their unique cultural tapestry, rooted in a history that blends Indigenous heritage, French and British colonial legacies, and a diverse immigrant population. This identity, while marked by pride in its multiculturalism and progressive values, also carries a certain reluctance when it comes to being absorbed into a larger political entity, particularly one as dominant and powerful as the United States.

For many Canadians, the idea of joining the U.S. is inherently tied to a loss of national sovereignty. The Canadian ego, at its core, is built on a distinctiveness that is not merely geographical but deeply cultural and political. Canada's social policies such as universal healthcare, its commitment to peacekeeping, and its reputation for embracing diversity have often set it apart from its southern neighbor. To consider merging with the United States would be to risk diluting those values, potentially losing the balance that Canadians have spent centuries forging between their European roots and their North American reality.

Public opinion in Canada, as of the last few decades, has overwhelmingly rejected the idea of becoming part of the United States. According to various polling data, fewer than 10% of Canadians have expressed interest in such a union. This reluctance speaks to the ego of a nation that values its independence and self-definition. Canadians are protective of their status as a middle power in the world, respected for its diplomacy, commitment to internationalism, and progressive stance on many global issues. Even with shared borders, language, and economic ties, Canada's sense of self is anchored in its autonomy, a feature that would undoubtedly be eroded if it were to join the U.S.

The American Ego: A Sense of Exceptionalism

On the other side of the border, the American ego is rooted in a historical narrative of exceptionalism, a belief that the United States is unique in its vision of democracy, freedom, and global leadership. The concept of American exceptionalism has been a cornerstone of U.S. political ideology for centuries. The idea that the U.S. represents the pinnacle of individual freedom, capitalist success, and democratic governance is so ingrained that it often clouds the willingness to entertain scenarios where the American way might be influenced or altered by another nation.

From an American perspective, incorporating Canada could be seen as a symbolic affirmation of that exceptionalism, reflecting the U.S.'s role as the dominant power in the Western Hemisphere. Yet, this same ego could lead to resistance, as Americans may not see the need to merge with a country they view as smaller, with a less aggressive political culture, and with economic and social systems that are sometimes at odds with their own.

Furthermore, the practical implications of merging with Canada would challenge America's sense of identity. The idea of incorporating a country with a distinct political and cultural heritage could be perceived as a dilution of American values. Public opinion in the U.S. has similarly been skeptical of the notion of adding another state, with polls showing that only a small portion of the American people, perhaps 20% at most, might entertain such an idea. This reflects a deeper ambivalence about openness to foreign influence and a willingness to engage in a partnership that could challenge the nation's identity.

The Role of Knowledge and Openness: Understanding the "Other"

Despite these ingrained egos, there is also an element of knowledge and openness in the Canadian American relationship that cannot be overlooked. The two countries share not only the world's longest undefended border but also a history of cooperation, trade, and mutual respect. In terms of economic ties, the U.S. and Canada are deeply intertwined, with the U.S. being Canada's largest trading partner and vice versa. Both nations benefit from this relationship, and that economic interdependence could provide a foundation for further integration.

In terms of culture, there is a surprising amount of openness on both sides of the border. The Canadian media landscape is flooded with American content, from Hollywood films to TV shows, and Canadian music, literature, and political figures are a regular presence in the American public sphere. Similarly, Canadians are often receptive to American ideas and innovations, from the latest technological advancements to political discourse. This cultural exchange, while not without its tensions, suggests that the two nations do have the capacity to understand one another and perhaps even evolve together, if not merge.

In an age where globalization is reshaping the way nations think about their borders; some Canadians and Americans may find it easier to imagine a more unified political and economic system. However, this knowledge of one another's systems and the shared understanding of each nation's cultural and political complexity would require time, dialogue, and a great deal of compromise. Open-mindedness would be essential in overcoming the deep-seated reservations both countries hold about merging into one.

Willingness to Merge: The Roadblocks

Ultimately, the most significant roadblock to the merging of the U.S. and Canada lies in the willingness of both peoples to see themselves as part of a larger political entity. Canadians are unlikely to want to relinquish their sovereignty, and Americans may be resistant to the idea of incorporating a large country with different social policies, particularly in areas like healthcare, gun control, and foreign relations.

Yet, in the face of global challenges such as climate change, economic instability and geopolitical conflicts, there may be growing conversations about how to best align policies between countries that share so much in common. The political will required to overcome these challenges and make such a radical transformation possible would require more than just political leaders. It would require a groundswell of public support, something that is currently lacking on both sides of the border.

Canada's openness to working alongside the U.S. in global affairs, trade, and regional security, as well as America's recognition of Canada's role as a stabilizing force in the Northern Hemisphere, may however, lay the groundwork for greater cooperation in the future. However, the idea of a full political union remains a distant possibility, driven more by abstract thought than concrete public demand.

A Thought-Provoking Exercise

In the end, the idea of Canada becoming the 51st state may remain just that, an unlikely thought experiment. However, it forces us to ask important questions about national identity, political sovereignty, and the willingness of nations to reshape their futures. Would such a union compromise or enhance the political and cultural values of both countries? Could the U.S. and Canada overcome the egos that define their respective identities, and find common ground for a deeper, more unified partnership?

While it is unlikely that this merger will become a reality in the foreseeable future, the very thought of it reminds us of the complexities of nationalism, the fragility of borders, and the power of shared history and values. Even if Canada and the United States do not merge into a single nation, the discussion itself serves as a reminder of the potential for collaboration and change in an increasingly interconnected world. The political future of both nations, whether as separate entities or as something more, will continue to be shaped by their knowledge, openness, and willingness to confront their evolving roles on the world stage.

Chapter 2

An Introduction to the History of the Concept

The idea of Canada becoming the 51st state of the United States is a notion that has been debated and explored for decades. While some may view this concept as a radical and unlikely scenario, others see it as a natural progression of the already deeply intertwined relationship between the two nations. As we consider the possibility of Canada joining the United States, it is essential to understand the dynamics between the two countries and the complexities that would arise from such a union.

Canada and the United States share the world's longest international border, spanning over 8,891 kilometers, 5,525 miles. The two nations have a long history of cooperation, trade, and cultural exchange, with the U.S. being Canada's largest trading partner. The bilateral relationship is built on a foundation of shared values, geographic proximity, and economic ties. The two countries have a significant impact on each other's economies, with the U.S. accounting for approximately 75% of Canada's exports.

The existing relationship between Canada and the United States is multifaceted, with cooperation extending beyond trade and commerce. The two nations have a strong partnership in defense and security, with joint efforts in counterterrorism, cybersecurity, and border security. They also collaborate on environmental issues, such as climate change, and have a long-standing agreement on the management of shared water resources.

Despite the close relationship, Canada has maintained its sovereignty and distinct identity. The country has a unique cultural heritage, shaped by its history, geography, and linguistic diversity. Canada's federal system of government, parliamentary democracy, and social policies, such as universal healthcare, also set it apart from its southern neighbor.

The concept of Canada becoming the 51st state is not new, with discussions dating back to the 19th century. However, recent events, such as the increasing globalization of trade, the rise of nationalist movements, the COVID-19 pandemic, and the election of President Donald Trump in November of 2024 have reignited the debate. Proponents of Canadian American union argue that it would bring economic benefits, enhanced security, and increased global influence. On the other hand, opponents contend that it would lead to a loss of Canadian identity, autonomy, and social programs.

The History and Possible Motives of Donald Trump with Regards to Canada Becoming the 51st State
Throughout his career, Donald Trump has not seriously pursued or advocated for the notion of Canada joining the United States. His rhetoric has typically centered on economic, trade, and immigration issues, particularly within the context of U.S.-Canada relations, but never to the extent of promoting formal statehood for Canada.

It is important to note that the idea of Canada becoming the 51st state remains highly speculative and theoretical, with little historical or political momentum in that direction. While Trump has expressed views on strengthening U.S.-Canada

relations and renegotiating trade deals like NAFTA, which evolved into the USMCA under his administration, the question of Canadian statehood has never been part of his political platform or policy agenda.

Since November 2024, after the U.S. presidential election, Trump has largely remained involved in political discourse, media appearances, and discussions related to the future of the Republican Party and his ongoing influence in U.S. politics. His focus has been on domestic issues, party leadership, and his legal challenges rather than any substantive proposals regarding the political future of Canada.

Given that the concept of Canada becoming the 51st state is not an element of mainstream political discussion, it might be unlikely that Trump or any significant American politician has made it a priority.

Although Donald Trump's views on Canada becoming the 51st state have not been part of his official political platform or public policy proposals, he has planted the seed for discussion and debate leading up to the beginning of his second term as President of the United States. There are elements of his rhetoric and his presidency that touch on the concept of deepening relations with Canada. The notion of Canada joining the United States as the 51st state is more of a hypothetical scenario that could be speculated upon, rather than something explicitly pursued by Trump during his time in office.

However, understanding Trump's general political philosophy, his views on U.S.-Canada relations, and his overarching goals can provide insight into why some might speculate about his motives or desire for such a union.

The notion of the United States annexing Canada as its 51st state has surfaced periodically when president elect Donald Trump suggested such a possibility. This proposal, though dismissed as an impossibility by Canadian leaders, raises questions about the legal and historical precedents for such an action.

Historical Context: War Plan Red

In the 1930s, the U.S. developed "War Plan Red," a secret military strategy outlining a potential invasion of Canada in the event of a conflict with the British Empire. The plan detailed various military offensives, including the capture of key Canadian cities and infrastructure. However, this plan was never enacted, and the U.S. and Canada have since maintained a peaceful and cooperative relationship.

Constitutional Considerations: Article II, Section 2

The U.S. Constitution, in Article II, Section 2, grants the President the power to make treaties, provided two-thirds of the Senate concurs. Therefore, any formal annexation of Canada would require a treaty between the two nations, necessitating approval from both the U.S. Senate and the Canadian government. Given Canada's strong national identity and sovereignty, such an agreement appears highly improbable for the near future.

Political and Legal Challenges

Beyond constitutional requirements, the annexation of Canada would face significant political and legal obstacles. Canadian Prime Minister Justin Trudeau and other leaders have firmly rejected the idea, emphasizing Canada's sovereignty and the unlikelihood of such a merger.

Additionally, the cultural, legal, and political differences between the two countries would pose substantial challenges to any integration efforts.

While historical documents like War Plan Red and constitutional provisions outline theoretical pathways for annexation, the practical, legal, and political barriers render the prospect of Canada becoming the 51st U.S. state exceedingly unlikely. The strong national identities and sovereignties of both nations, coupled with the complexities of such an undertaking, suggest that this idea will remain a hypothetical scenario rather than a reality.

Donald Trump's Approach to International Relations and Nationalism

One of the key elements of Donald Trump's presidency was his "America First" ideology. This philosophy prioritized American interests in every aspect of governance, from trade deals to foreign relations. Trump's approach to international relations was characterized by skepticism toward multilateral organizations and global agreements, as well as a preference for bilateral agreements that favored U.S. economic and political dominance.

Trump's "America First" rhetoric often led him to challenge international partnerships and alliances, favoring policies that benefited the U.S. economy directly. His presidency was marked by actions such as pulling out of the Paris Climate Agreement, questioning the value of NATO, and renegotiating trade deals like NAFTA, which became the USMCA, the United States-Mexico-Canada Agreement. His stance on Canada within the context of trade, particularly during the renegotiation of NAFTA, was confrontational, with Trump repeatedly criticizing Canada for what he saw as unfair trade practices, particularly regarding dairy exports and tariffs on American goods.

Trump's skepticism of Canada, while rooted in his "America First" ideology, did not extend to the idea of Canadian annexation. In fact, Trump is unlikely to have publicly or privately advocated for Canada to become the 51st state. However, the broader context of his views on trade, sovereignty, and relationships with neighboring countries suggests that he saw value in having a closer, more controlled relationship with Canada, but not necessarily by formal annexation.

Hypothetical Motives Behind Supporting Canadian Statehood

Even though Trump never directly pushed for Canada to become the 51st state, hypothetically, there are several motives that could explain why someone with his political philosophy might entertain or be supportive of such a notion.

Economic Integration

Trump's primary goal throughout his presidency was to ensure that the U.S. economy was competitive and growing. Canada's integration as a state would create an even larger, more unified North American economic bloc, which could be appealing in terms of consolidated markets, resources, and industries. Canada's vast natural resources, such as oil, timber, and minerals, could offer economic advantages to the U.S. economy, with the added benefit of easier access to these resources and no trade barriers between the two nations.

Trade and Resources

Trump's stance on trade was often transactional. Canada is already one of the U.S.'s largest trading partners, and any trade disputes between the two countries, such as disagreements over dairy tariffs or softwood lumber, were handled within a complex bilateral framework. By integrating Canada as a state, Trump could imagine eliminating such trade disputes altogether and removing tariffs, making resource exchange, trade deals, and economic activity much more efficient.

Security and Global Influence

Another possible motive for Trump's hypothetical support of Canada's statehood would be enhancing U.S. security and influence. The U.S. and Canada already share a long border and have close military cooperation through organizations like NATO and NORAD, North American Aerospace Defense Command. The formal integration of Canada into the United States would streamline defense policies, joint military efforts, and security cooperation, further cementing North America's global strength. For a leader like Trump, who valued military strength and global dominance, the integration of a large, resource-rich neighbor would likely appeal to him in terms of strengthening the U.S.'s position on the world stage.

Historical Context and Trump's Previous Comments on Canada

While Trump has not pushed for Canada to become the 51st state, his rhetoric on Canada has sometimes been characterized by hostility or dissatisfaction, especially during trade negotiations. However, he also had moments of praise for the relationship between the two countries, particularly regarding shared interests in security. For example, during the 2018 renegotiation of NAFTA, Trump famously referred to Canada as "very tough" in negotiations, and he made frequent remarks about how Canada was engaging in practices that were, in his view, unfair to American businesses. These comments were seen as part of his broader campaign to renegotiate trade agreements in favor of U.S. interests.

However, Trump has also expressed admiration for certain aspects of Canada. In 2017, Trump praised Canada's commitment to economic cooperation, even as he criticized certain policies. His relationship with Canadian Prime Minister Justin Trudeau was sometimes strained but did feature moments of mutual respect, particularly in their shared interest in NAFTA renegotiation.

Why Trump Would or Wouldn't Want Canada as the 51st State

Although it's easy to speculate about what Trump might want from such a drastic political shift, it is important to consider why he likely would not have pushed for Canada's statehood.

Donald Trump has never officially called for Canada to become the 51st state, but he has made several offhand remarks or comments over the years that have fueled speculation about his views on the idea. These comments are often made in a lighthearted or exaggerated manner, with Trump joking about Canada's natural resources, political alignment, or geographical proximity to the U.S.

Trump's rhetoric sometimes includes making provocative statements for effect, but there is no formal policy proposal from him to make Canada part of the U.S. Such a move would be politically and constitutionally complex, requiring substantial legal changes and the approval of both U.S. and Canadian governments, which is highly challenging.

Any statements on this matter seem more like political banter or strategic comments rather than a genuine proposal.

While there is no evidence of Trump seriously advocating for Canada to become a U.S. state, there are a few reasons why he has made joking or rhetorical comments about it in the past. These reasons tend to align with his political style or views on the U.S. and its neighboring countries:

Geopolitical and Economic Interests

Trump has often emphasized the importance of strong economic ties with neighboring countries, including Canada. He might make comments about integrating Canada because of its proximity and valuable resources, such as oil and natural gas, which Trump has previously mentioned in discussions about energy independence.

Shared Ideology

Trump has occasionally suggested that the U.S. and Canada are ideologically aligned in some ways, especially on issues like trade, business, and security. He may have alluded to the idea of a closer political union as a way to strengthen these areas.

Nationalism

Trump's America First agenda has sometimes led to remarks about expanding U.S. influence in North America. In some ways, his desire to exert more control over the region, particularly when it comes to trade deals like the USMCA (formerly NAFTA), has fueled discussions about greater integration.

Joking or Hyperbole

Many of Trump's comments about Canada seem to be exaggerated or made in jest. He often uses humor or bold rhetoric to spark discussion or provoke reactions. In this sense, his comments could be seen as a way to engage audiences with an eye-catching, albeit non-serious, idea.

While these reasons help explain why Trump might make such comments, there is no indication that he has an official plan to push for Canada becoming the 51st state. Nonetheless, President Trump's comments have made many Canadians uneasy and many others hopeful of seeing such a merger.

Preserving U.S. Sovereignty

Trump's political platform was centered on American sovereignty and self-reliance. His "America First" agenda often focused on limiting the influence of foreign entities, whether through international organizations like the United Nations or trade agreements like NAFTA. Adding Canada as the 51st state would effectively dilute U.S. sovereignty by introducing a new political and cultural context. While the idea of closer economic relations with Canada may have appeal, the practical integration of Canadian governance and the preservation of U.S. supremacy within the country's borders may conflict with Trump's ideological stance on national sovereignty.

Domestic Political Challenges

The political landscape of the United States would likely be resistant to such a drastic change. Even if Trump had supported the idea of integrating Canada as a state, it could face massive opposition from both major political parties. There would be concerns over how the U.S. political system would accommodate the addition of new states, the creation of new congressional districts, and the integration of Canadian laws, languages, and social systems into the U.S. structure.

Cultural and Regional Differences

Trump's vision for America was one that prioritized cultural cohesion and a unified national identity. While Canada shares many economic and cultural similarities with the U.S., there are significant differences, particularly in terms of language, such as French in Quebec, national identity, and social policies such as universal healthcare. For many Americans, the inclusion of Canada as a state could present challenges to maintaining a coherent national identity, which would run counter to Trump's focus on American exceptionalism.

In conclusion, Donald Trump's public rhetoric regarding Canada becoming the 51st state has been largely hypothetical, and there is little evidence to suggest he pursued such an agenda during his presidency. However, if he had been interested in the idea, his motives would likely have been shaped by his broader political philosophy, namely, his desire for economic strength, political control, and global dominance under the "America First" ideology. While the formal integration of Canada would have offered opportunities for resource consolidation and trade efficiency, Trump's political strategy and emphasis on U.S. sovereignty could likely make the idea of annexing Canada a difficult and controversial proposition. Thus, while Trump may have spoken favorably of closer ties with Canada, the notion of it becoming the 51st state was more of a speculative idea rather than an actual goal for his administration.

This book will explore the complexities of Canada becoming the 51st state, examining the historical context, economic implications, cultural considerations, and political feasibility of such a union. We will delve into the potential benefits and drawbacks, as well as the perspectives of various stakeholders, including Canadians, Americans, and international observers. Through a comprehensive analysis, we will aim to provide a nuanced understanding of this intriguing idea and its potential consequences for both nations

In the following chapters, we will:

Examine the historical context of Canadian American relations and the evolution of the idea of Canada becoming the 51st state

Analyze the economic implications of a potential union, including trade, investment, and labor market effects

Discuss the cultural considerations, including the impact on Canadian identity, language, and social policies

Investigate the political feasibility of a union, including the necessary steps, potential roadblocks, and stakeholder perspectives

Explore the international implications of a Canadian American union, including the reactions of other nations and potential effects on global governance

Discuss the possible process of the union, including the referendum and obtaining public approval

By exploring these aspects, we hope to provide a comprehensive understanding of the possibilities and challenges associated with Canada becoming the 51st state, shedding light on the complexities of this intriguing idea.

Chapter 3
A Brief History of Canada-US Relations

The relationship between Canada and the United States is one of the most significant and enduring in the world. The two countries share a long border, a common language, and a history of cooperation and mutual respect. However, the idea of Canada becoming the 51st state of the United States is a complex and contentious issue that has been debated by scholars, politicians, and the public for many years.

To understand the context of this debate, it is essential to examine the history of Canada-US relations. The relationship between the two countries has evolved over time, shaped by a series of key events and milestones that have had a profound impact on Canadian and American society.

One of the earliest and most significant events in the history of Canada-US relations was the American Revolution. The Revolution marked a turning point in the relationship between the two countries, as the newly independent United States began to assert its claims to territory that is now part of Canada. The Treaty of Paris, signed in 1783, established the border between the United States and British North America, which would eventually become Canada.

Throughout the 19th century, the relationship between Canada and the United States continued to evolve. The War of 1812, fought between the United States and the British Empire, had a significant impact on the development of Canada, as it led to an increase in British immigration and investment in the region The construction of the Canadian Pacific Railway, completed in 1885, further solidified the connection between Canada and the United States, as it provided a vital transportation link between the two countries.

In the 20th century, the relationship between Canada and the United States became even more intertwined. The two countries fought together in both World War I and World War II, and the United States played a significant role in shaping Canada's foreign policy during the Cold War. The establishment of the North American Aerospace Defense Command, NORAD, in 1958 marked a significant milestone in the development of Canada-US relations, as it provided a framework for cooperation on defense and security issues.

Despite the many positive developments in Canada-US relations, there have also been periods of tension and conflict. The Vietnam War, for example, marked a significant low point in the relationship, as many Canadians opposed the United States' involvement in the conflict. The election of Donald Trump as President of the United States in 2016 also marked a significant shift in the relationship, as Trump's policies on trade and immigration had a major impact on Canada.

In recent years, the idea of Canada becoming the 51st state of the United States has gained significant attention. While some have argued that this would be a positive development, others have expressed concerns about the potential impact on Canadian sovereignty and identity. Shark Tank's Kevin O'Leary, for example, has suggested that half of Canadians are interested in becoming the 51st state, citing the potential economic benefits of such a move.

However, others have argued that the idea of Canada becoming the 51st state is not a realistic or desirable option. Pete McMartin, for example, has suggested that the United States should consider making Canada its 11th province, rather than the 51st state, citing the many cultural and economic ties between the two countries. Since becoming president elect in 2024, Donald Trump has also joked about Canada joining the United States, suggesting that it would be a good idea for both countries. That joke has now become a usual rhetoric of Trump, leading both Canadians and Americans to the believe that this 51st state could possibly become a reality.

Chapter 4
The Benefits of a Union

As the prospect of Canada becoming the 51st state gains momentum, it is essential to examine the potential benefits of such a union. In this chapter, we will delve into the economic, political, and social advantages of Canada joining the United States, as well as the potential impact on trade, security, and cultural exchange.

Economic Benefits

One of the most significant advantages of Canada becoming the 51st state is the potential for economic growth. As a member of the United States, Canada would gain access to a massive market of over 330 million consumers, providing a significant boost to its economy. The elimination of trade barriers and tariffs would facilitate the exchange of goods and services, creating new opportunities for Canadian businesses to expand and thrive.

According to a study by the Canadian American Business Council, a union between Canada and the United States could lead to an increase in bilateral trade of up to 20%, resulting in an estimated $100 billion in additional economic activity. This, in turn, could lead to the creation of thousands of new jobs and a significant increase in economic output.

Furthermore, Canada's natural resources, including oil, gas, and timber, would become an integral part of the United States' energy and resource mix, providing a secure and reliable source of energy for the country. This could lead to significant investments in Canada's energy sector, creating new opportunities for economic growth and development.

Political Benefits

A union between Canada and the United States could also have significant political benefits. As a member of the United States, Canada would gain a seat at the table in international affairs, allowing it to play a more prominent role in global politics. This could lead to increased influence and credibility for Canada on the world stage, enabling it to more effectively promote its interests and values.

Additionally, a union would provide Canada with access to the United States' extensive diplomatic network, allowing it to leverage the country's relationships with other nations to advance its own foreign policy objectives. This could be particularly beneficial in regions where Canada has limited diplomatic presence, such as the Middle East and Asia.

Social Benefits

The social benefits of a union between Canada and the United States are also significant. As a member of the United States, Canada would gain access to a wide range of programs and services. This could lead to improved living standards and quality of life for Canadians, particularly in areas such as healthcare, where the United States has a more comprehensive and well-funded system.

Furthermore, a union would provide Canadians with the opportunity to live and work in the United States, allowing them to take advantage of the country's diverse cultural and economic opportunities. This could lead to increased mobility and flexibility for Canadians, enabling them to pursue their goals and aspirations in a wider range of contexts.

Impact on Trade

According to a study by the U.S. Chamber of Commerce, a union between Canada and the United States could lead to an increase in bilateral trade of up to 30%, resulting in an estimated $150 billion in additional economic activity. This could lead to significant investments in industries such as manufacturing, agriculture, and energy, creating new opportunities for economic growth and development.

Impact on Security

A union between Canada and the United States could also have a significant impact on security. As a member of the United States, Canada would gain access to the country's extensive military and defense capabilities, providing a secure and reliable source of protection for its citizens.

This could be particularly beneficial in areas such as counterterrorism and cybersecurity, where the United States has significant expertise and resources. A union would also provide Canada with the opportunity to participate in international security initiatives, such as NATO, allowing it to play a more prominent role in global security affairs.

Impact on Cultural Exchange

Finally, a union between Canada and the United States would have a significant impact on cultural exchange between the two countries. As a member of the United States, Canada would gain access to a wide range of cultural institutions and programs, including museums, galleries, and performance venues.

This could lead to increased collaboration and exchange between Canadian and American artists, writers, and musicians, enriching the cultural landscape of both countries. A union would also provide Canadians with the opportunity to participate in American cultural events and festivals, allowing them to experience the country's vibrant cultural scene firsthand.

In conclusion, the potential benefits of Canada becoming the 51st state are significant and far-reaching. From economic growth and job creation to increased influence and credibility on the world stage, a union between Canada and the United States could have a profound impact on the country's future. As we continue to explore the possibilities of a union, it is essential to carefully consider the potential advantages and disadvantages, ensuring that any decision is made with the best interests of citizens in mind.

The idea of Canada and the United States becoming something akin to the European Union (EU) is an interesting thought experiment, but some would argue, highly unlikely for several reasons. The EU is a unique political and economic union, with its own set of rules, shared currency (the Euro), and political institutions designed to ensure cooperation across diverse member states with different histories, languages, and cultures. Here are some factors that make such an arrangement between Canada and the U.S. improbable:

Political Sovereignty

Canada and the U.S. are both independent sovereign nations with their own political systems, constitutions, and foreign policies. While they share close cultural, political, and economic ties, especially through agreements like the USMCA (formerly NAFTA), both countries value their sovereignty. Merging or creating a political union similar to the EU would require significant constitutional changes, national referenda, and an agreement to give up some degree of sovereignty, which is unlikely to be politically acceptable to citizens or leaders in either country.

Cultural and Social Differences

While Canada and the U.S. share a lot of cultural similarities, they also have important differences, such as healthcare systems, public in Canada vs. largely private in the U.S., political ideologies, and historical identities. Canada has a strong sense of its distinct national identity, including its multicultural policies and bilingual nature, French and English, which could make integration difficult for many Canadians.

Economic Systems

Both countries have economies that are heavily integrated, but their economic models differ in important ways. For example, Canada has a more regulated and publicly funded healthcare system, while the U.S. relies on private healthcare. Economic policies, taxation, and the role of government in the economy vary between the two nations, which could make economic integration challenging without major changes to how both countries operate.

Public Opinion

Public opinion in both countries would likely play a significant role in preventing any move toward a political union. Canadians generally value their independence and are proud of their national identity. While there is strong support for maintaining close relations with the U.S., the idea of merging into a single political entity would likely be met with resistance. Similarly, while some in the U.S. might appreciate the economic benefits of closer ties, most would not support the political changes that would be required.

International Implications

Canada and the U.S. are both members of many international organizations, including the United Nations, NATO, and the World Trade Organization. Becoming a single political entity would alter their global standing, alliances, and obligations. For example, Canada has a different approach to foreign policy and peacekeeping, which might conflict with U.S. military interventions or diplomatic approaches.

Legal and Constitutional Barriers

Both the U.S. and Canada would face enormous legal and constitutional hurdles. In the U.S., the Constitution would need to be amended, which requires significant political consensus, something unlikely to happen given the political divisions in the country. Canada's constitution would also need to be rewritten to accommodate such a major shift in its national identity.

Historical Context

Historically, the U.S. and Canada have had moments of tension and separation, such as the War of 1812 and disagreements over territory, although their relationship has been overwhelmingly peaceful since then. Nevertheless, Canada's history as a former British colony has given it a strong sense of independence, which it continues to value.

While Canada and the U.S. already have a strong relationship in terms of trade, defense, and cultural exchange, the idea of them becoming a political union similar to the EU is very unlikely. The countries would have to overcome deep political, economic, cultural, and constitutional challenges to even consider such an arrangement.

Chapter 5
The Drawbacks of a Union

As the possibility of Canada becoming the 51st state of the United States continues to be debated, it is essential to consider the potential drawbacks of such a union. While there may be benefits to joining the United States, there are also significant economic, political, and social disadvantages that must be taken into account. In this chapter, we will examine the potential drawbacks of union and consider the impact on Canadian sovereignty, identity, and autonomy.

Economic Disadvantages

One of the primary concerns about Canada becoming the 51st state is the potential economic impact. While the United States is a global economic powerhouse, Canada's economy is significantly smaller and more vulnerable to fluctuations in the US market. As a result, Canada may find itself subject to US economic policies that are not in its best interests.

Loss of Economic Sovereignty

As a state, Canada would be required to adopt US economic policies, including tax laws, trade agreements, and monetary policy. This would lead to a loss of economic sovereignty, as Canada would no longer have control over its own economic destiny.

Increased Dependence on the US

Canada's economy is already heavily dependent on the US, with a significant portion of its trade going to its southern neighbor. As a state, Canada would become even more integrated into the US economy, making it vulnerable to economic downturns in the US.

Potential for Economic Instability

The US economy is known for its volatility, with frequent boom and bust cycles. As a state, Canada would be exposed to these fluctuations, which could lead to economic instability and uncertainty.

Political Disadvantages

In addition to economic concerns, there are also significant political drawbacks to Canada becoming the 51st state.

Loss of Political Sovereignty

As a state, Canada would be required to adopt US laws and policies, which could lead to a loss of political sovereignty. Canada would no longer have control over its own laws, regulations, and policies.

Reduced Representation

As a state, Canada would have limited representation in the US Congress, with only two senators and a handful of representatives in the House of Representatives. This would give Canada limited influence over US policy, despite being a significant contributor to the US economy.

Potential for Conflict

The US and Canada have a long history of cooperation, but there are also significant differences between the two countries. As a state, Canada may find itself at odds with the US government on issues such as healthcare, education, and foreign policy.

Social Disadvantages

Finally, there are also social disadvantages to consider when evaluating the potential drawbacks of Canada becoming the 51st state.

Loss of Cultural Identity

Canada has a unique cultural identity that is distinct from the US. As a state, Canada may find its cultural identity eroded, as it becomes more integrated into the US.

Potential for Social Unrest

The integration of Canada into the US could lead to social unrest, as Canadians may feel that their way of life is being threatened.

Impact on Indigenous Communities

Canada has a significant indigenous population, with many communities having their own distinct cultures and traditions. As a state, Canada may find its indigenous communities negatively impacted by US policies, which could lead to social unrest and conflict.

Loss of Sovereignty: As a state, Canada would no longer be a sovereign nation, with control over its own laws, policies, and economy.

Erosion of Identity

The integration of Canada into the U.S. could lead to an erosion of Canadian identity, as Canada becomes more Americanized.

Reduced Autonomy

As a state, Canada would have limited autonomy, with the US government having significant influence over Canadian policy and decision-making.

While there may be benefits to Canada becoming the 51st state, there are also significant drawbacks to consider. The economic, political, and social disadvantages of union could have a profound impact on Canadians. As Canadians consider their future, it is essential to carefully weigh the pros and cons of union and consider what is best for their country.

Recommendations

Based on the analysis presented in this chapter, the following recommendations could be made:

Careful Consideration

Canadians and Americans should carefully consider the pros and cons of union.

Economic Impact Assessment

An economic impact assessment should be conducted to determine the potential economic effects of union.

Political Representation

Canadians should consider the potential for reduced representation in the US Congress and the impact on Canadian influence over U.S. policy.

Cultural Identity

Canadians and Americans should consider the potential impact on cultural identity and take steps to preserve and promote it.

Indigenous Communities

The potential impact on indigenous communities should be carefully considered, and steps should be taken to ensure that their rights and interests are protected.

By carefully considering the potential drawbacks of union and taking steps to mitigate them, Canadians can make an informed decision about their future and ensure that their country remains strong and prosperous.

Future Research Directions

Further research is needed to fully understand the potential drawbacks of Canada becoming the 51st state. Some potential areas of research could include:

Economic Modeling

Economic modeling could be used to simulate the potential economic effects of union in Canada and the U.S.

Public Opinion Research

Public opinion research should be conducted to determine the views of Canadians on the potential drawbacks of union.

Comparative Analysis

A comparative analysis could be conducted to compare the experiences of other countries that have joined the US as states.

Policy Analysis

A policy analysis could be conducted to determine the potential impact of US policies on Canada. By conducting further research, Canadians and Americans can gain a deeper understanding of the potential drawbacks of union and make a more informed decision about their future.

By carefully weighing the pros and cons of union and taking steps to mitigate the potential drawbacks, Canadians and

Americans can ensure that their country remains strong and prosperous. Further research is needed to fully understand the potential drawbacks of union, and both Canadians and Americans should approach this decision with caution and careful consideration.

Chapter 6
The Constitutional Implications

The possibility of Canada becoming the 51st state of the United States raises a multitude of constitutional implications that would need to be carefully considered and addressed. The integration of a new state into the American federal system would require significant changes to both the Canadian and American constitutions. In this chapter, we will examine the potential constitutional implications of such a union and discuss the possible changes that could need to be made to both countries' foundational documents.

An Introduction to Constitutional Implications

The constitution of a country is its supreme law, outlining the framework of government, the powers of various branches, and the rights of citizens. When two countries with different constitutional frameworks consider merging, the constitutional implications can be far reaching and complex. In the case of Canada becoming the 51st state, both the Canadian and American constitutions would need to be amended to accommodate the new relationship.

The Canadian Constitution

The Canadian Constitution, also known as the Constitution Act, 1867, is the foundation of Canada's federal system. It outlines the powers of the federal government, the provinces, and the territories, as well as the rights of Canadian citizens. If Canada were to become the 51st state, significant changes would need to be made to the Canadian Constitution to ensure compatibility with the American federal system.

One of the primary concerns would be the division of powers between the federal government and the provinces. In Canada, the provinces have significant autonomy and powers, whereas in the United States, the federal government has more authority. The Canadian Constitution would need to be amended to reflect the new balance of power and ensure that the provinces' rights are protected.

Another area of concern would be the Canadian Charter of Rights and Freedoms, which is enshrined in the Canadian

Constitution. The Charter guarantees fundamental rights and freedoms to Canadian citizens, including freedom of speech, equality, and protection from unreasonable search and seizure. The American Bill of Rights, on the other hand, has some differences in its provisions and interpretations. The Canadian Charter would need to be reconciled with the American Bill of Rights to ensure consistency and protection of individual rights.

The American Constitution

The United States Constitution, adopted in 1787, is the foundation of the American federal system. It outlines the framework of government, the powers of the various branches, and the rights of American citizens. If Canada were to become the 51st state, changes would need to be made to the American Constitution to accommodate the new state.

One of the primary concerns would be the representation of Canada in Congress. The American Constitution would need to be amended to provide for Canadian representation in both the House of Representatives and the Senate. This would require adjustments to the apportionment of seats and the electoral college system.

Another area of concern would be the incorporation of Canadian laws and institutions into the American federal system. The American Constitution would need to be amended to recognize and incorporate Canadian laws, courts, and institutions, ensuring a smooth transition and minimizing disruptions to the existing system.

Potential Changes to the Canadian and American Constitutions

To accommodate Canada as the 51st state, both the Canadian and American constitutions would need to undergo significant changes. Some potential changes that could be considered include:

Repeal of the Canadian Constitution

One possible approach would be to repeal the Canadian Constitution and replace it with a new constitution that is compatible with the American federal system. This would require a significant overhaul of the Canadian constitutional framework and could be a complex process.

Amendments to the Canadian Constitution

Alternatively, the Canadian Constitution could be amended to reflect the new relationship with the United States. This would require changes to the division of powers, the

Canadian Charter of Rights and Freedoms, and other provisions to ensure compatibility with the American federal system.

Amendments to the American Constitution

The American Constitution would also need to be amended to accommodate Canada as the 51st state. This could require changes to the representation of Canada in Congress, the incorporation of Canadian laws and institutions, and other provisions to ensure a smooth transition.

Impact on the Canadian Charter of Rights and Freedoms

The Canadian Charter of Rights and Freedoms is a cornerstone of Canadian democracy, guaranteeing fundamental rights and freedoms to Canadian citizens. If Canada were to become the 51st state, the Charter would need to be reconciled with the American Bill of Rights to ensure consistency and protection of individual rights.

Some potential implications for the Canadian Charter include:

Repeal of the Charter

One possible approach would be to repeal the Canadian Charter and replace it with the American Bill of Rights. This would require significant changes to the Canadian constitutional framework and could be a complicated process.

Amendments to the Charter

Alternatively, the Canadian Charter could be amended to reflect the new relationship with the United States. This would require changes to the provisions of the Charter to ensure compatibility with the American Bill of Rights.

Incorporation of the Charter into the American Bill of Rights

Another approach could be to incorporate the Canadian Charter into the American Bill of Rights, ensuring that the rights and freedoms guaranteed to Canadian citizens are protected and preserved.

The constitutional implications of Canada becoming the 51st state are complex and far reaching. Both the Canadian and American constitutions would need to undergo significant changes to accommodate the new relationship. The division of powers, representation in Congress, and the incorporation of Canadian laws and institutions would all need to be addressed. The Canadian Charter of Rights and Freedoms would also need to be reconciled with the American Bill of

Rights to ensure consistency and protection of individual rights. Ultimately, the success of such a union would depend on the ability of both countries to navigate these complex constitutional implications and create a new framework that works for all citizens.

In conclusion, the constitutional implications of Canada becoming the 51st state are complex and multifaceted. Both the Canadian and American constitutions would need to undergo significant changes to accommodate the new relationship. The success of such a union would depend on the willingness and ability of both countries to navigate these complex constitutional implications and create a new framework that works for all citizens.

Chapter 7
The Role of the Monarchy

The question of Canada becoming the 51st state of the United States raises a multitude of complex issues, one of which is the role of the monarchy in Canada. As a constitutional monarchy, Canada has a long history of association with the British Crown, and the monarch serves as the head of state. In this chapter, we will examine the role of the monarchy in Canada, its relationship with Canadians, and the potential implications for the monarchy if Canada were to become the 51st state.

The Role of the Monarchy in Canada

In Canada, the monarch serves as the head of state, but their role is largely symbolic and ceremonial. The monarch's representative in Canada is the Governor General, who is appointed by the monarch on the advice of the Canadian Prime Minister. The Governor General performs many of the duties of the head of state, including signing bills into law, appointing judges and other officials, and representing Canada abroad.

Despite the limited role of the monarch in Canadian politics, the institution of the monarchy remains an important part of Canadian identity and culture. Many Canadians see the monarchy as a connection to their country's history and heritage, and the monarch is often seen as a unifying figure who represents the nation as a whole.

The Relationship between the British Monarch and the Canadian State

The relationship between the British monarch and the Canadian state is quite complex. The monarchy has played a significant role in shaping Canadian identity and culture. From the Queen's image on Canadian currency to the monarch's role in Canadian ceremonies and traditions, the monarchy is an integral part of Canadian life.

While many Canadians see the monarchy as a symbol of their country's history and heritage, others view it as a relic of a bygone era, one that is no longer relevant to modern Canada.

On the one hand, the monarch serves as the head of state for Canada, and the Canadian government is responsible for advising the monarch on matters related to Canada. On the other hand, the British monarch is also the head of state for the United Kingdom, and the UK government has its own relationship with the monarch.

In practice, this means that the Canadian government has a significant degree of autonomy in its dealings with the monarch, but the UK government also has a role to play in certain matters, such as the appointment of the Governor General. This relationship is governed by a set of complex rules and conventions, including the Statute of Westminster, which granted dominion status to Canada in 1931.

Potential Implications for the Monarchy if Canada were to become the 51st State

If Canada were to become the 51st state of the United States, the implications for the monarchy would be significant. In all likelihood, the monarchy would cease to play a role in Canadian politics, and the head of state would become the President of the United States.

This would require significant changes to the Canadian constitution, including the abolition of the office of the Governor General and the transfer of the monarch's powers to the President. It would also require changes to the Statute of Westminster, which would need to be amended or repealed to reflect Canada's new status as a state within the United States.

The loss of the monarchy would also have cultural and symbolic implications for Canada. Many Canadians would likely feel a sense of loss and disconnection from their country's history and heritage, and the monarch would no longer serve as a unifying figure for the nation.

On the other hand, some Canadians might see the abolition of the monarchy as an opportunity to create a new and more modern system of government, one that is more in line with the values and principles of the United States. This could involve the creation of a new head of state, such as a president or chancellor, who would serve as the symbol of Canadian identity and unity.

The Future of the Monarchy in a Unified North America

In the event that Canada was to become the 51st state, it is possible that the monarchy could continue to play a role in some form. For example, the monarch could continue to serve as a symbol of Canadian identity and culture, even if they were no longer the head of state.

Alternatively, the monarchy could be abolished altogether, and a new system of government could be established that is more in line with the values and principles of the United States. This would require significant changes to the Canadian constitution and the Statute of Westminster, but it could also provide an opportunity for Canada to create a new and more modern system of government.

Ultimately, the future of the monarchy in a unified North America would depend on a variety of factors, including the terms of the union, the wishes of the Canadian and American people, and the policies of the governments involved. However, one thing is certain: the role of the monarchy in Canada would be significantly altered, and the implications for Canadian identity and culture would be profound.

The Monarchy and Canadian History

The monarchy has played a significant role in Canadian history, from the earliest days of British colonization to the present day. The monarch has served as the head of state for Canada, and the institution of the monarchy has been an integral part of Canadian politics and culture.

In the event that Canada was to become the 51st state, the monarchy's role in Canadian history would likely be significantly altered. The monarch would possibly no longer serve as the head of state, and the symbolism of the monarchy could be lost.

Consultation with the Canadian People

Ultimately, the future of the monarchy in a unified North America could be determined by the Canadian people. It might be recommended that a national referendum or consultation be held to determine the wishes of Canadians regarding the monarchy. Nonetheless, it is possible to ensure that the monarchy continues to play a meaningful role in Canadian culture and identity, even if Canada were to become part of the United States.

Future Research Directions

Future research on the role of the monarchy in Canada and its potential impact on union could possibly focus on the following areas:

The Relationship between the Monarchy and Canadian Identity

Further research might be needed to understand the complex relationship between the monarchy and Canadian identity. This could involve studies of Canadian attitudes towards the monarchy, as well as analysis of the role of the monarchy in Canadian culture and history.

The Impact of Union on the Monarchy

Further research could also be necessary to understand the potential impact of union on the monarchy. This could involve studies of the implications of union for the monarch's role in Canadian politics, as well as analysis of the potential changes to the Canadian constitution and the Statute of Westminster.

The Future of the Monarchy in a Unified North America

Further research may also be needed to understand the potential future of the monarchy in a unified North America. This could involve studies of the potential role of the monarch in a unified North America, as well as analysis of the implications of union for Canadian culture and identity.

By pursuing these research directions, it is possible to gain a deeper understanding of the complex relationship between the monarchy and Canadian identity, and to develop a more nuanced understanding of the potential implications of union for the monarchy.

In conclusion, while the monarchy serves as the head of state, the institution of the monarchy is also an integral part of Canadian culture and identity.

In the event that Canada was to become the 51st state, the implications for the monarchy would be significant. The monarch would likely cease to play a role in Canadian politics, and the symbolism of the monarchy would be lost.

However, it is also possible that the monarchy could continue to play a role in Canadian culture and identity, even if Canada were to become part of the United States. Ultimately, the future of the monarchy in a unified North America would depend on a variety of factors, including the terms of the union, the wishes of the people, and the policies of the governments involved.

Chapter 8
The Potential Effects on the Provinces and Territories

The prospect of Canada becoming the 51st state of the United States raises a myriad of complex questions about how such a hypothetical union would impact the individual provinces and territories that make up the Canadian Confederation. Each province and territory has its own distinct political, economic, and cultural characteristics, and the ramifications of joining the U.S. would vary significantly depending on their circumstances. Would some regions stand to benefit from the change, while others might lose? To answer this, we must examine how the unique features of each province and territory could influence their reactions to the potential union.

British Columbia

British Columbia, with its strategic position on the Pacific Rim, could stand to gain significantly from expanded economic opportunities if Canada were to become the 51st state. The province's robust trade networks with Asia and its thriving technology and film industries could flourish under a larger and more integrated U.S. market. The alignment with American economic policies might also attract additional investment in infrastructure and innovation.

However, these economic gains would come with potential environmental concerns. British Columbia's pristine natural landscapes, including its forests, rivers, and coastlines, could face increased pressure from U.S. resource extraction policies and infrastructure development.

British Columbia (BC) is one of Canada's most economically vibrant provinces, with a thriving tech sector, a major film industry, and extensive natural resources. As part of the U.S., British Columbia could see substantial economic growth, benefiting from seamless access to U.S. markets and increased trade opportunities. However, British Columbia's progressive political culture might clash with certain conservative policies in the U.S., particularly in areas like environmental regulation and healthcare.

Economic Opportunities

With its proximity to Pacific trade routes and tech hubs like Vancouver, British Columbia could leverage its position to become an even more central player in the U.S. economy. Its rich natural resources, particularly in forestry and energy, would be valuable assets.

Political Tension

British Columbia's liberal values on issues like climate change and social services might find resistance in the U.S. political landscape. It could also face challenges navigating the transition from Canada's single payer healthcare system to the U.S.'s complex and varied health insurance models.

Alberta

Alberta is a province defined by its oil sands, agricultural industry, and a strong conservative political identity. As the U.S. 51st state, Alberta could possibly find more alignment with American energy policies, particularly with the development of fossil fuels. We will discuss the Alberta Question in more detail in an upcoming chapter.

Saskatchewan

Saskatchewan, a province rich in agriculture and natural resources, would likely find economic opportunities in joining the U.S. markets, particularly in agriculture and energy.

Economic Expansion

As part of the U.S., Saskatchewan's agriculture sector could benefit from better trade agreements, access to U.S. markets, and a more stable currency. Saskatchewan's rich mineral deposits would also be attractive to the U.S. economy.

Healthcare Issues

Saskatchewan's health care system, as in all provinces and territories, emphasizes universal public health. Perhaps a merger would force Canadians to transition to a more fragmented U.S. healthcare system. This could lead to challenges for many residents accustomed to the Canadian model.

Manitoba

Manitoba's economy is diverse, with significant contributions from agriculture, manufacturing, and the service sector. Its integration into the U.S. could provide economic advantages, though the potential loss of Canadian social policies may cause concern.

Economic Opportunities

Manitoba could benefit from easier access to U.S. markets and better trade relations with its southern neighbor. Industries such as aerospace and agriculture could grow, especially given the province's proximity to the U.S. Midwest.

Social Concerns

Like other provinces with robust social systems, the loss of Canada's universal healthcare and social safety nets could lead to dissatisfaction. The shift from Canadian public programs to U.S. private alternatives might be viewed unfavorably by residents who value public services.

Ontario

Ontario is Canada's economic powerhouse, home to major financial hubs like Toronto and important manufacturing industries. The province's economy would experience significant changes under U.S. governance, but its global status could be enhanced.

Financial Integration

Ontario's major financial services industry would benefit from integration into the U.S. economy, particularly with closer links to Wall Street. Its manufacturing sector would also benefit from greater access to U.S. markets, though competition could increase.

Political and Cultural Identity

Ontario's relatively progressive policies and multicultural character might clash with certain aspects of American conservatism. Its large immigrant population would also need to navigate a new immigration system, which might be more restrictive than Canada's.

Quebec Identity Struggles and Cultural Integration

Quebec's relationship with the rest of Canada has always been marked by its distinct French heritage, and the province has a unique place within Canadian society due to its language, culture, and political aspirations. Joining the U.S. would introduce new challenges for Quebec's identity, language, and political autonomy.

Cultural Erosion

Quebec's most significant concern would be the erosion of its Francophone identity. The province has fiercely protected its French language and culture, and joining the U.S. could undermine these protections. The U.S. has no official language, and the predominance of English could marginalize French speakers in Quebec.

Loss of Political Power

Quebec would likely lose its political leverage on the Canadian federal stage, as its influence would be diluted within the broader U.S. political system, where it might struggle to maintain its cultural and political distinctiveness.

Quebec's unique French speaking identity would create challenges in the event of integration into the U.S. Despite this, Quebec has a strong economy, particularly in aerospace, technology, and energy, which could benefit from the move.

Cultural and Linguistic Challenges

Quebec's French speaking population and distinct culture could face significant challenges in a country where English is dominant. Quebec's historical separatist movement would complicate its relationship with the rest of the U.S., potentially leading to tensions about cultural preservation and language rights.

Economic Integration

Quebec's economy, particularly in high tech industries like aerospace, could thrive within the larger U.S. market. However, the province's relatively strong government intervention in the economy may clash with U.S. federal economic policies that favor a more market-driven approach.

We will discuss the Quebec Question in more detail in an upcoming chapter.

New Brunswick

New Brunswick's economy relies heavily on natural resources, particularly forestry and mining, as well as agriculture. As part of the U.S., the province could see both opportunities and challenges related to its trade relationships and natural resource policies.

Economic Opportunities

The province would benefit from more favorable trade agreements, potentially expanding its access to U.S. markets. New Brunswick's position on the U.S.-Canada border could make it an important logistics hub.

Social Services

New Brunswick's reliance on federal transfer payments from the Canadian government might face difficulties, as the U.S. federal system doesn't provide similar redistributive payments. This could strain social services in the province.

Nova Scotia

Nova Scotia, with its emphasis on fisheries, tourism, and a growing technology sector, would likely see a mixed impact from joining the U.S.

Economic Growth

Nova Scotia's tourism industry could see an uptick from more integrated travel systems with the U.S., while its growing tech sector could benefit from U.S. investment and trade relationships.

Political Adjustments

Like other smaller provinces, Nova Scotia might feel the loss of provincial autonomy, especially when it comes to policies related to healthcare and social services.

Prince Edward Island

As Canada's smallest province, Prince Edward Island (PEI) has a population heavily reliant on agriculture and tourism. Being integrated into the U.S. would present economic challenges but also opportunities for growth.

Agricultural Integration

Prince Edward Island's agricultural exports would benefit from easier access to U.S. markets. However, U.S. agricultural policies might pose challenges, particularly regarding tariffs and subsidies for smaller producers.

Cultural Identity

The loss of Canadian identity could be deeply felt in a province with such a small population, where local culture is highly valued. Prince Edward Island would also face the challenge of integrating into a larger and more diverse national system.

Newfoundland and Labrador

Newfoundland and Labrador are geographically isolated and rely on oil, mining, and fisheries. Its economic ties with the U.S. would likely deepen but concerns about the loss of Canadian identity and services might linger.

Economic Integration: The province could benefit from its proximity to U.S. markets and resources, especially in the oil and gas industry. Increased access to U.S. investment and markets could boost Newfoundland's economic growth.

Social and Political Adjustment

Newfoundland's progressive values on issues like healthcare and social welfare would likely conflict with U.S. policies, especially in a region that faces persistent challenges with economic inequality.

The Territories (Yukon, Northwest Territories, Nunavut)

Canada's northern territories have unique challenges due to their remote locations, small populations, and dependence on natural resources and federal support. Transitioning to

U.S. statehood could require intense consideration of the distinct needs of these regions.

Economic Impact

The territories' economies rely heavily on mining, oil, and government transfers. The integration into the U.S. economy could provide increased investment, particularly in resource extraction, but it might also leave people living in the territories vulnerable to U.S. federal policies that do not always prioritize remote regions.

Social Support

The loss of Canada's generous federal transfers could result in significant social and economic challenges. The territories would need to adapt to the different healthcare, education, and welfare systems in the U.S., which might not align with the needs of these sparsely populated regions.

The integration of Canada as the 51st state of the United States would be an unprecedented transformation with profound effects on each province and territory. While economic opportunities could abound, the social, political, and cultural implications of such a move could be complex. The diverse needs and identities of each region would shape how they navigated this new reality, with challenges to unity, identity, and governance. The prospect of such a union, while intriguing, would require careful and nuanced consideration for each part of Canada.

Chapter 9
The Quebec Question

In an alternate reality where Canada becomes the 51st state, Quebec stands at the center of a complex and evolving identity. In this version of history, the language divide between English and French speakers becomes one of the most defining and turbulent aspects of potential Canadian American unity. This chapter delves into the centuries long struggle between English and French speakers in Canada and imagines the future of Quebec as it navigates this newly united political landscape. How would Quebec's distinct cultural and linguistic identity fare in a federal system, where its voice would need to compete for influence within the broader framework of an American union?

In this narrative, the story of Quebec's history, from its colonial roots under the French to its tumultuous relationships with the English speaking serves as a backdrop for understanding the complexities of this imagined future. As we explore the impact of this monumental change, we will discuss how Quebec's quest for recognition and autonomy interacts with the broader American political experiment.

The Legacy of the Conquest

The history of Quebec as a French colony dates back to the early 1600s, when Samuel de Champlain established the first permanent French settlement in North America. French speaking settlers known as Canadiens began to carve out a new life in the fertile lands along the St. Lawrence River. However, in 1763, following the Seven Years' War, the Treaty of Paris handed over control of New France to Britain, creating a deep fissure in the nascent Canadian identity. English speaking settlers poured into the territory, transforming the demographic makeup of what would later become Canada.

The Conquest of New France left a lingering resentment among French speaking Quebecois. While the British allowed the French to retain their language, religion, and civil law, a tension between the two cultural groups persisted. English speaking elites controlled most economic and political power, while French Canadians were relegated to a subordinate position in the societal hierarchy.

As Quebec would later discover, the language divide created not only cultural tension but also a fundamental power imbalance that would fuel future conflicts.

The Quiet Revolution and the Rise of Nationalism

Fast-forward to the mid-20th century, when Quebec's growing sense of nationalism reached a boiling point. The Quiet Revolution of the 1960s marked a shift toward modernization, secularization, and political activism. Under the leadership of figures like Jean Lesage, the province began to reject the traditional political and religious establishment. The Liberal government's modernization policies sought to elevate the French speaking majority, creating institutions like the Ministry of Education and Hydro-Québec, which played pivotal roles in both the economy and the province's cultural life.

Simultaneously, the rise of separatist movements such as the Parti Québécois (PQ) transformed Quebec's political landscape. For many, the idea of a distinct French-Canadian state free from English speaking dominance became a unifying dream. The Parti Québécois won power in 1976, with René Lévesque leading the charge for independence.

This was the beginning of a period of intense political struggle that would define Quebec's place in Canada.

Despite efforts to create a "sovereign" Quebec, including a controversial 1980 referendum on separation, Quebec remained a part of Canada. The failure to secede in 1980 didn't quell the separatist movement; rather, it galvanized it. In 1995, another referendum on Quebec's sovereignty would narrowly fail by a mere 1% but the underlying dissatisfaction among Quebec's French speaking population was undeniable.

The Canada-United States Merger

In this alternative future, we consider the hypothetical scenario where Canada, including Quebec, eventually joins the United States as its 51st state. This decision could have been spurred by a range of factors, including economic pressures, the exhaustion of the Quebec sovereignty movement, and the need for a united front to face the challenges of globalization. The merger would likely spark a wave of debates over Quebec's place in the new political framework, particularly concerning language rights, cultural preservation, and political autonomy.

Would Quebec's French speaking population be able to maintain its linguistic and cultural identity under the

American system? Or would the homogenizing forces of American federalism overwhelm Quebec's unique status? These are critical questions in understanding the future of Quebec in the 51st state.

Language Politics in a Federal Union

Language has always been at the heart of Quebec's identity. In a Canada-United States union, the question of language would be among the first to surface. English is the dominant language in the United States and Canada, but French has a longstanding presence in Quebec, with significant implications for daily life, education, and business.

In this scenario, Quebec would likely push for strong protections for the French language, similar to the language laws that exist in Canada today. The language issue would not only shape Quebec's internal politics but also its relationship with the other 50 states. Federal policies around bilingualism, education, and language rights would likely be a critical need for maintaining Quebec's distinct cultural heritage.

Would French be recognized as an official language of the new 51st state, or would it be relegated to a minority status, as it often was in Canadian federal politics? Could a compromise be reached where French was preserved in

Quebec, while English remained the language of the broader union? These tensions would reflect a larger question of cultural assimilation versus preservation.

Cultural and Economic Impact

Quebec's cultural life, including its celebrated art, film, and culinary traditions would also face new challenges in the broader American context. The province's unique culture, much of which is rooted in its French heritage, could find itself at odds with the dominant Anglo American cultural norms. However, this could also present an opportunity for Quebec to play a leading role in the growing global Francophone community.

Economically, Quebec would bring its significant industries, including aerospace, technology, and hydroelectric power, into the larger American system. Would Quebec's economy benefit from the integration, or would it be absorbed by larger American corporations, leading to a dilution of its distinct economic base? Would Quebec's welfare state policies, including universal healthcare and a robust public sector, survive in the more market oriented American system?

The tension between economic pragmatism and cultural preservation would shape Quebec's future trajectory in the potential union of Canada and the U.S.A.

In the 1970s and 1980s, Quebec experienced significant political, social, and economic changes, particularly with the rise of the sovereignty movement and efforts to preserve and promote the French language and culture. These developments ultimately led to a shift in economic power from Quebec, particularly Montreal, to Ontario, with Toronto emerging as the dominant economic hub. The key reasons behind this shift can be attributed to the following factors:

The Rise of Quebec Nationalism and Language Laws

One of the most important political developments in Quebec during the 1970s and 1980s was the rise of the *Parti Québécois* (PQ), which advocated for Quebec's sovereignty and the protection of the French language and culture. The sovereignty movement culminated in two referendums, one in 1980 and another in 1995, both of which saw a significant portion of Quebec's population vote for independence though both referendums were ultimately unsuccessful.

In the 1970s, the Bill 101, also known as the Charter of the French Language, was passed by the PQ government under

Premier René Lévesque. This law made French the official language of Quebec and imposed strict language requirements on businesses, education, and government.

Businesses were required to operate primarily in French. Public signage had to be in French, with English only signs becoming increasingly restricted. The law restricted access to English language schools, requiring children of immigrants and francophone parents to attend French language schools unless one of their parents had attended English language school in Quebec.

These policies were intended to strengthen Quebec's French language culture and identity. However, they also created significant economic and social tensions, particularly with English speaking communities, French families that would have preferred that their children attended English schools and businesses that had long thrived in Montreal.

Impact on Montreal's Business Community

Montreal had been the economic powerhouse of Canada throughout much of the 20th century. It was a major financial, commercial, and industrial center with a vibrant English speaking business community. However, as Quebec's language laws tightened and the sovereignty movement gained momentum, many businesses and professionals began to leave Montreal for more economically stable and less politically uncertain environments. This was due to several reasons:

Uncertainty about Quebec's Future

The rising tide of separatism and the fear that Quebec might eventually become independent created a sense of insecurity among both local and international businesses. Many executives, investors, and companies feared the potential for political instability or the complications of doing business in a province with such an uncertain future.

Language Laws and Restrictions

The enforcement of Bill 101 made it more difficult for English speaking businesses and professionals to operate in Quebec. Companies that relied on English as the primary language of communication found it increasingly difficult to comply with the law, especially in terms of advertising, customer relations, and hiring practices. Since English was often seen as the international language for business, Quebec was often seen as an inappropriate place for businesses to thrive. Many, then opted to leave Quebec.

Immigration and Talent Drain

The emphasis on French language and culture in Quebec also led to a decline in the influx of English-speaking immigrants, who were often crucial to the city's economy. Many people with valuable business experience and skills chose to move to Toronto, where English was the dominant language and there were fewer restrictions on language and culture.

The Economic Shift to Ontario and Toronto

As Montreal's business community began to fragment and move out of Quebec, Toronto emerged as the primary beneficiary of this shift. There were several key factors driving this economic migration to Ontario:

Toronto's Economic Growth

During the 1970s and 1980s, Toronto was already a growing financial and commercial center, and it was rapidly becoming the economic heart of Canada. The city's real estate, banking, technology, and manufacturing sectors boomed, attracting both domestic and international investment. The increasing political uncertainty in Quebec, combined with the rising cost of doing business in Montreal, made Toronto a much more attractive option for businesses.

Political Stability

Ontario, with its more moderate political environment and commitment to bilingualism but without the pressure of language laws like in Quebec, provided a much more stable and predictable environment for businesses. This political stability, particularly in contrast to Quebec's political tensions, made it an attractive location for companies and investors seeking security.

Ontario became easier for companies to expand, hire talent, and establish themselves in a business-friendly environment. Toronto's infrastructure, including its world class financial institutions, transportation networks, and access to international markets, made it a natural choice for both Canadian and foreign companies.

Corporate Headquarters and Finance
Major corporations, including banks, insurance companies, and manufacturers, began to relocate their headquarters or major operations from Montreal to Toronto. The banking sector, in particular, was heavily impacted, with major financial institutions like the Bank of Montreal and the Royal Bank of Canada shifting their focus to Toronto, further consolidating the city's position as Canada's financial capital.

The Long-Term Impact on Montreal and Quebec's Economy

While Montreal did not lose all of its economic strength, it certainly experienced a significant decline in its status as Canada's financial hub. By the 1980s and 1990s, Montreal had lost its position as the country's primary business center to Toronto. The shifting economic landscape also had a long-term impact on Quebec's broader economy, as the province became more dependent on public sector employment and industries such as aerospace and technology.

However, Montreal has since reinvented itself, particularly in the tech, cultural, and creative sectors, and remains a key player in Canada's economy, though it is no longer the dominant hub it once was.

Quebec's Political Identity in a U.S. State

Given Quebec's history and cultural stronghold on maintaining their French language, its position as a political entity within the American union would be complicated, to say the least. The cost of protecting the French language, however negative the financial impact on the province, would influence the merger of Canada and the U.S. Would Quebec remain a political powerhouse, with a distinct voice in Congress? Or would the province's political weight diminish in a federal system dominated by larger states?

Would the history of Quebec's struggle for autonomy, from the patriot uprisings of the 1830s to the debates over national identity in the 20th century, carry forward into the new political landscape? As Quebec adjusted to being part of the United States, questions of political representation, taxation, and self-rule would spark ongoing debates.

Would Quebec's distinct political traditions, such as its preference for a strong social safety net and its advocacy for the French language be preserved, or would it be forced to compromise in order to maintain unity with the rest of the U.S.?

Quebec's Future as the 51st State

Quebec's role in a hypothetical union with the United States presents a provocative and multifaceted question: Can Quebec retain its cultural and linguistic identity in a political landscape dominated by English speaking North America? Or would the province be subsumed by the overwhelming influence of the broader American union?

Quebec's rich history, shaped by centuries of French and English linguistic and cultural conflict, would undoubtedly continue to shape its future. Whether as an integral part of the 51st state or as a province that defines the very meaning of multiculturalism, Quebec could remain an essential part of the narrative with the United States.

The balance between unity and diversity would ultimately determine whether Quebec could flourish in the American political framework or whether the province's distinctiveness would be too strong a force for a united federation to bear.

Chapter 10
The Alberta Debate

Alberta's vast plains, towering mountains, and abundant natural resources have long been a source of pride and contention within Canada. If Canada had ever joined the United States as its 51st state, Alberta's unique economic, political, and cultural landscape would have faced a new, complex challenge in navigating a federal system dominated by its southern neighbor. One of the most defining issues in Alberta's history has been its oil wealth, a resource that has both fueled its prosperity and deepened its divisions with the rest of Canada.

This chapter explores how Alberta's resource driven economy, particularly its oil sands and energy sector, would play a central role in the politics of a unified North America. It will examine how Alberta's historical struggles with the federal government over resource development, fiscal policy, and political autonomy could shift in the context of a new, American style union. Alberta's quest for greater economic independence and control over its oil wealth could continue to shape its political identity in a broader American framework, and the balance of power between Alberta and the rest of the states would be a pivotal aspect of the imagined future.

Alberta's Founding and Early Economic Struggles

When Alberta joined Canada in 1905, it was a relatively young province, its economy largely built on agriculture, forestry, and natural resources. Its vast oil and gas potential was not yet discovered, and its economic structure was firmly aligned with the broader national policies of the Canadian government. However, it wasn't long before the province began to grow, and the land that would later become known as Alberta's "oil sands" began to attract attention.

In the early 20th century, Alberta's economy was largely controlled by Eastern Canada, particularly the financial capital of Montreal, Quebec. The west was often seen as a raw frontier, an agricultural heartland with limited financial clout in the decisions made in Ottawa. Alberta's relationship with the rest of Canada was strained by its feeling of being sidelined in the national economic vision, a sentiment that would only grow as the province began to develop its own resources.

The Discovery of Oil and the Beginning of Alberta's Energy Dominance

In the 1940s, Alberta's oil industry began to take shape. The discovery of the Leduc oil field in 1947 marked a new era for the province. Alberta had struck "black gold," and its role in the Canadian economy would never be the same again. Over the following decades, oil would become Alberta's economic lifeblood, propelling it from a relatively small agricultural province into one of Canada's wealthiest regions.

However, Alberta's newfound oil wealth also sowed the seeds of tension between the province and the rest of Canada. The national government, based in Ottawa, increasingly sought to control the country's oil and gas resources, implementing policies that aimed to centralize power over energy in federal hands. The conflict over control of Alberta's natural resources reached its peak in the 1970s and 1980s, when nationalization and federal energy programs were proposed to ensure a fairer distribution of wealth and resources across the country.

Alberta's response to these federal moves was clear: it wanted to retain control over its own oil. The rise of Alberta Premier Peter Lougheed in the 1970s highlighted the growing desire for provincial autonomy, particularly in the management and development of its oil reserves. Lougheed's leadership was marked by resistance to federal encroachment on Alberta's economic sovereignty, culminating in the province's fight against the National Energy Program (NEP), which was perceived by many Albertans as an unjust policy that benefited the rest of Canada at their expense.

The National Energy Program and the Seeds of Discontent

The National Energy Program, introduced by the federal government in 1980, remains one of the most controversial chapters in Alberta's history. In an effort to control rising oil prices and ensure more equitable energy distribution, the federal government implemented the National Energy Program, which imposed higher taxes on Alberta's oil and gas production and sought to redistribute wealth to the rest of Canada. For Alberta, the NEP was seen as a direct attack on its economic interests and a blatant overreach by a central government.

The National Energy Program sparked widespread protests in Alberta, leading to the rise of a populist movement that championed Alberta's independence. Many Albertans viewed the program as an unfair tax on their prosperity, and the resentment towards Ottawa deepened. The province felt betrayed by the federal government, which was seen as failing to recognize the unique economic realities of Alberta.

While the National Energy Program was eventually dismantled, the damage was done. The seeds of Western alienation were sown, and Alberta's relationship with the rest of Canada, particularly in terms of resource management, would never be the same. This tension over oil wealth and control would persist into the 21st century, culminating in calls for greater provincial autonomy or even independence.

Alberta's Oil Economy in the Context of a United States of Canada

If Canada joined the United States as its 51st state, Alberta may face a new set of challenges. In the American federal system, resource management is largely the responsibility of the states, and Alberta's oil reserves would likely have become an important part of the national energy landscape. But the question remains: would Alberta be able to maintain its control over its own resources, or would it find itself subsumed by the power dynamics of a larger, more influential American economy?

Alberta's oil wealth could undoubtedly make the province a key player in the energy sector. However, as part of the United States, Alberta would likely face pressure to align its policies with national energy goals, which could conflict with the province's desire to maximize profits from its oil sands. The possibility of a more decentralized American system could allow Alberta more autonomy over its energy resources, but the influence of multinational corporations and American political forces could introduce new dynamics into Alberta's energy politics.

The financial ramifications of this shift could be profound. Alberta's economy is built on oil exports, and as part of the United States, it may need to navigate a new set of trade agreements, taxes, and regulations. Would Alberta's oil remain the province's primary economic driver, or would the broader economic forces of the U.S. overwhelm Alberta's local industries? How would Alberta's wealth be distributed in this new framework, and would the province's economic strength be diluted or amplified?

Financial Tensions and the Struggle for Political Autonomy

One of the key issues Alberta has historically faced is the financial disparity between it and other provinces. While Alberta is one of the wealthiest provinces in Canada, it has often been at odds with the federal government's equalization payments system, which redistributes wealth from richer provinces to poorer ones. Alberta has long argued that it contributes more to the Canadian economy than it receives in return, a point that has fueled its sense of political and economic disenfranchisement.

By Canada becoming the 51st state, this issue would likely persist. Alberta would still face the reality of contributing a disproportionate share of national resources, while its wealth might be used to support states with less developed economies. The question of fiscal fairness would be central to Alberta's relationship with the other 50 states, and the province's desire for greater control over its economic destiny would likely push for a redefined system of resource revenue sharing.

A Changing Landscape: Alberta's Role in North America

In a united North America, Alberta would continue to be a major player in the energy sector. Its oil sands are among the largest untapped reserves in the world, and its natural resources would likely be a cornerstone of the continent's energy future. However, Alberta's role within the broader political and economic landscape would be shaped by its ability to navigate the challenges of integration into a larger federal system.

Would Alberta's political autonomy be protected in the face of increasing American influence? How would Alberta's deep-rooted populism and desire for self-determination fit into the American system of governance? Would Alberta's oil wealth continue to be a source of pride, or would the pressures of national politics dilute the province's unique identity?

As Alberta moves forward into a potential future as part of a United States, these questions will remain central to its trajectory. The province's relationship with oil, finance, and political power will continue to evolve.

Alberta's oil wealth, economic struggles, and political aspirations have shaped the province's identity and its relationship with the rest of Canada. If Canada became the 51st state, Alberta would probably face a radical political environment, one where the tensions over resource control, fiscal fairness, and provincial autonomy could continue to play a central role.

In the end, Alberta's future as part of the 51st state may hinge on its ability to assert its influence in a new political and economic context. Alberta would likely want to ensure that its energy driven prosperity continues to benefit its people, while preserving its unique identity within the broader North American union. The legacy of Alberta's oil economy and its ongoing struggle for economic independence could continue to shape the province's future, no matter where it stood in the 51st state.

Chapter 11

Indigenous Peoples and Union

The potential union of Canada with the United States as the 51st state has sparked intense debate and discussion among various stakeholders, including Indigenous peoples. As the largest and most diverse group of Aboriginal peoples in Canada, Indigenous peoples have a unique set of concerns and interests that must be considered in any discussion of union. This chapter will examine the potential impact of union on Indigenous peoples in Canada, discuss the historical and contemporary relationships between Indigenous peoples and the Canadian state, and consider the potential implications for Indigenous rights and self-government.

Historical Context

The relationship between Indigenous peoples and the Canadian state has often been complex. For centuries, Indigenous peoples have lived in Canada, with their own distinct cultures, languages, and traditions. However, with the arrival of European settlers, Indigenous peoples were subjected to colonization, displacement, and marginalization. The Indian Act of 1876, which remains in effect today, imposed a paternalistic and assimilationist policy on Indigenous peoples, restricting their rights and freedoms.

In recent years, there have been efforts to reconcile and redress the historical injustices perpetrated against Indigenous peoples. The Truth and Reconciliation Commission of Canada, established in 2008, documented the experiences of Indigenous peoples in residential schools and made recommendations for reconciliation and healing. The Canadian government has also established the Inquiry into Missing and Murdered Indigenous Women and Girls, which aims to address the disproportionate rates of violence and disappearance among Indigenous women and girls.

Potential Impact of Union

The potential union of Canada with the United States as the 51st state could have significant implications for Indigenous peoples. On one hand, union could provide opportunities for increased economic development and access to resources, which could benefit Indigenous communities. On the other hand, union could also lead to the erosion of Indigenous rights and self-government, as well as the loss of cultural identity and autonomy.

The Canadian government has recognized Indigenous rights to land through various treaties and agreements, such as the Treaty of Niagara and the Numbered Treaties. However, these rights are not necessarily recognized by the United States, which has its own set of laws and policies governing Indigenous lands and rights. If Canada were to become the 51st state, it is unclear how these rights would be affected, and whether Indigenous peoples would be able to maintain their current level of autonomy.

Another concern is the potential impact of union on Indigenous cultural identity and language. Indigenous languages and cultures are an essential part of Canadian identity and are recognized and protected through various laws and policies, such as the Official Languages Act and the Canadian Multiculturalism Act. However, if Canada were to become part of the United States, it is unclear how these languages and cultures would be recognized and protected, and whether they would be subject to the same level of marginalization and erasure as Indigenous languages and cultures in the United States.

Implications for Indigenous Rights and Self-Government

The potential union of Canada with the United States as the 51st state raises significant implications for Indigenous rights and self-government. One of the primary concerns is the potential erosion of Indigenous rights to land and self-government, as well as the loss of cultural identity and autonomy. If Canada were to become part of the United States, it is unclear how these rights would be affected, and whether Indigenous peoples would be able to maintain their current level of autonomy and self-government.

Indigenous self-government is recognized and protected through various laws and policies, such as the Sechelt Indian Band Self-Government Act and the Cree-Naskapi of Quebec Act. However, if Canada were to become part of the United States, it is unclear how these laws and policies would be affected, and whether Indigenous self-government would be recognized and protected to the same extent.

To address these concerns, it may be important that any discussion of union takes into account the unique needs and interests of Indigenous peoples. This could include recognizing and respecting Indigenous rights to land and self-government, as well as protecting Indigenous cultural identity and language. It could also require meaningful consultation and engagement with Indigenous peoples, to ensure that their voices and perspectives are heard and respected throughout the process.

In conclusion, the potential union of Canada with the United States as the 51st state has significant implications for Indigenous peoples. While union could provide opportunities for increased economic development and access to resources, it also raises concerns about the erosion of Indigenous rights and self-government, as well as the loss of cultural identity and autonomy. To address these concerns, it is important that any discussion of union considers the unique needs and interests of Indigenous peoples and recognizes and respects their rights to land and self-government. Ultimately, the decision to pursue union should be made with the full and informed consent of Indigenous peoples in order to protect their rights and interests.

Chapter 12
The Impact on Canadian Culture: A New Era of Integration and Transformation

The notion of Canada joining the United States as its 51st state presents profound questions about cultural preservation and transformation. Over the course of its history, Canada has developed a unique cultural identity rooted in its vast geography, bilingual heritage, Indigenous roots, and the complex interplay between its English and French speaking populations. What would become of these cultural distinctions in a federal system dominated by the United States? Would Canada's rich cultural mosaic be subsumed by American norms and ideals, or would the country's identity find new avenues of expression within a broader North American framework?

In this chapter, we will examine the potential impact of Canada's union with the U.S. on Canadian culture, particularly in the realms of arts, literature, and media. We will also explore the larger question of Canadian identity: Would Canadians continue to see themselves as distinct from their southern neighbors, or would the unification of the two countries create a shared North American identity?

The Changing Landscape of Canadian Culture

Canada's culture has always been shaped by its geographic vastness and diversity. From the multicultural cities of Toronto and Vancouver to the French speaking heart of Quebec, to the traditions of Indigenous communities across the country, Canada has cultivated an identity that is simultaneously collective and uniquely regional. The very nature of Canadian culture is one of balance between French and English heritage, between Indigenous and settler narratives, and between the urban and rural.

If Canada were to become the 51st state, this delicate balance would likely face significant pressures. The U.S. cultural framework is built on the notion of a unified identity, heavily shaped by American exceptionalism, consumer capitalism, and the omnipresence of popular culture. It is possible that the mosaic like diversity that defines Canada could be overshadowed by the more homogenizing influence of

American cultural values. This could affect various aspects of Canadian society, from everyday interactions to the way people perceive themselves on the global stage.

In a united political entity, the interplay between Canadian and American cultures would undoubtedly spark a process of negotiation and integration. While some elements of Canadian culture such as French-Canadian traditions, Indigenous cultural practices, and regional music might continue to thrive in specific communities, the overall narrative of "being Canadian" would face a re-evaluation. Would Canadians continue to identify as "Canadian" in the same way, or would the political union lead to the gradual blending of Canadian identity with that of its larger neighbor?

The Transformation of Canadian Arts and Literature

One of the most visible ways in which Canadian identity is expressed is through its arts and literature. Canadian writers, artists, filmmakers, and musicians have created works that explore the country's multiculturalism, its landscapes, and its dual linguistic heritage. The legacy of figures such as Margaret Atwood, Leonard Cohen, Alice Munro, and Michael Ondaatje is a testament to the unique literary and artistic traditions that have emerged from Canada's cultural mosaic.

If Canada became the 51st state, it's likely that the very foundation of Canadian arts and literature would shift. While many Canadian writers and artists have achieved international acclaim, particularly in English speaking countries, their works are often infused with themes that reflect Canada's national identity whether through the exploration of its history, its relationship with Indigenous peoples, or its bilingualism. Would these themes still resonate in the broader North American context, or would they be overshadowed by the more dominant cultural currents of the United States?

In the world of literature, for example, Canadian writers have long grappled with questions of national identity and how to define Canada's place in the world. From the "Canadian novel" to the exploration of the country's multicultural fabric, Canadian literature has been both a product of and a response to Canada's distinctiveness. As part of a larger American federation, Canadian writers might find it difficult to sustain their focus on national identity. Publishers, literary critics, and readers might increasingly look to American norms and genres, pushing Canadian authors to either conform to American literary traditions or adapt in ways that could dilute their unique cultural voice.

Similarly, in the realm of the arts, Canadian filmmakers and visual artists have often explored themes specific to Canada's history and geography. The success of films like *The Sweet Hereafter* (1997), *Atanarjuat: The Fast Runner* (2001), and *Bon Cop, Bad Cop* (2006) demonstrates how Canadian cinema often reflects the country's complex cultural tapestry. In a U.S. dominated media landscape, Canadian cinema might struggle for visibility on a larger stage, particularly as the American film industry, with its commercial dominance and deep ties to Hollywood continues to shape global entertainment.

Would Canadian artists find a way to continue celebrating and exploring their country's unique characteristics, or would the gravitational pull of American cultural norms dilute Canada's artistic expressions?

The Evolution of Canadian Media and Communication

Canada's media landscape has long been marked by its bilingual nature, the importance of public broadcasting such as the CBC, and the distinctiveness of its national news outlets. The idea of Canadian media reflects a hybrid of British influences, French heritage, and American proximity. Public broadcasters like the Canadian Broadcasting Corporation (CBC) have provided an avenue for Canadians to engage with their own culture, heritage, and political identity, often shaping how Canadians interact with both domestic and international events.

If Canada were to become the 51st state, Canadian media would likely undergo a major transformation. The presence of American media giants such as CNN, Fox News, and NBC already exerts a significant influence on Canadian culture, but the direct incorporation of Canada into the U.S. political system could lead to the further homogenization of media content. Canadian news outlets may increasingly align with American interests and narratives, reducing the distinctiveness of Canadian reporting.

Would the CBC continue to serve as a public service broadcaster, or would it be absorbed into a broader, American run national media framework? Would Canadian programming, which often reflects national concerns such as bilingualism, Indigenous issues, and Canadian politics continue to exist, or would it be phased out in favor of U.S. centric content?

Furthermore, Canadian entertainment outlets could face increasing competition from American television networks and streaming platforms. The strong pull of Hollywood, combined with the reach of global streaming services like Netflix and Disney+, could significantly reduce the production and consumption of homegrown Canadian content. Nationally supported initiatives to foster Canadian creativity and talent might be eroded in favor of globalized content that speaks to a broader North American audience.

While some Canadian artists and creators may embrace this larger platform, others could resist the growing tide of Americanization, seeking to retain the core elements of Canadian media that have given voice to the country's distinctive identity.

Canadian Identity and National Pride in a Unified North America

Perhaps the most profound shift that would result from Canada's integration into the United States would be the redefinition of Canadian identity. Canada has long prided itself on being a multicultural, bilingual, and peaceful country with a distinct national identity that sets it apart from the United States. This identity has been reinforced by Canada's historical narratives, symbols, and collective experiences, such as the peaceful resolution of the October Crisis, the recognition of Indigenous rights, and the cultural contributions of figures like Terry Fox and Leonard Cohen.

In a united political entity, the role of Canadian national pride would likely undergo a dramatic shift. Would Canadians continue to see themselves as distinct from their American counterparts, or would the common political structure of a 51st state lead to a dilution of Canadian identity? The notion of "being Canadian" has always been rooted in its differences such as its healthcare system, its bilingualism, its commitment to multiculturalism, and its distinct social values. As part of the United States, these elements could be overshadowed by American values, potentially leading to a loss of what made Canada unique in the first place.

On the other hand, some Canadians might embrace the opportunity to redefine their identity in a new context. A shared North American identity might emerge, characterized by an emphasis on economic prosperity, cultural exchange, and cooperation with the larger U.S. political and economic system. For some, the creation of a single, unified political and cultural entity could open new doors for cultural collaboration and influence on the global stage.

A New Chapter for Canadian Culture

If Canada were to become the 51st state, its cultural landscape would inevitably change, but the exact nature of that transformation is impossible to predict. Canadian arts, media, and national pride would undoubtedly evolve in response to the forces of Americanization, but the country's unique heritage, its bilingualism, its multiculturalism, and its commitment to regional diversity would continue to inform the debate over its future. Whether Canada's cultural identity would be absorbed into a larger North American whole or whether it would retain its distinctiveness within the American federation would depend on how deeply the values of Canadian culture could endure in the face of change.

What remains clear is that Canada's cultural journey, whether independent or part of a greater union, would continue to be one of reinvention, negotiation, and resilience. In this new North American era, the question of what it means to be Canadian would evolve, but the stories, traditions, and artistic expressions of the people would remain central to the country's ongoing narrative.

Chapter 13

The Impact on American Culture: A New North American Identity

The hypothetical union of Canada as the 51st state would also have far-reaching implications for American culture. The integration of a culturally distinct nation, with its own history, languages, traditions, and social norms, would not only alter the political landscape of North America but also reshape American cultural life in profound ways. Canada's inclusion in the United States would introduce new dynamics in the realms of arts, literature, media, and national identity, ultimately influencing how Americans perceive themselves and their place in the world.

In this chapter, we will explore the potential effects of Canada's accession on American culture, considering the ways in which Canada's diversity, history, and values would interact with and potentially transform American cultural norms. We will also delve into how American arts, literature, and media might shift as a result of this union and reflect on what this could mean for American national pride and identity.

The Changing Fabric of American Culture

American culture is often described as a product of assimilation, where diverse influences from immigrant populations, regions, and histories blend into a unique national identity. The idea of the "melting pot", though increasingly nuanced and debated, has long been a cornerstone of American cultural philosophy. The integration of Canada as the 51st state, however, would challenge this notion in fundamental ways, as Canada is not merely a part of the cultural mosaic, but a distinct entity with its own separate cultural and social foundations.

Canada's diverse population, which includes not only English and French speaking communities but also a large Indigenous presence and significant immigrant groups, would add new layers of complexity to the American cultural landscape. The introduction of a bilingual, French English, and multicultural society would prompt Americans to confront their own definitions of diversity. Canada's multicultural policies, which prioritize the integration of immigrants while respecting cultural differences, might influence future American immigration and diversity policies, potentially creating more room for diverse cultural expressions in mainstream society.

In urban areas across the U.S., the infusion of Canadian culture could lead to new cultural exchanges, collaborations, and innovations. Cities like New York, Chicago, and Los Angeles, already home to large expatriate populations, might witness a heightened blending of cultural influences in food, fashion, music, and public life. As Canadians bring their regional foods, celebrations, and traditions into American cities, there would likely be an expansion of multicultural festivals, bilingual spaces, and greater emphasis on recognizing diverse cultural histories.

However, such a cultural amalgamation could also face resistance. Some Americans, particularly those in regions with less exposure to Canadian influences, may perceive this union as a dilution of what it means to be "American." The tension between preserving traditional American cultural norms and accommodating a larger, more diverse populace could give rise to debates about cultural identity, assimilation, and the balance of power between national and regional values.

The Impact on American Arts, Literature, and Media

The arts and media have always played a pivotal role in shaping a nation's identity. If Canada were to join the United States, the artistic and literary landscapes would undergo a transformation as Canadian voices and influences became part of the broader American cultural conversation. This shift would have far-reaching consequences for American arts, literature, and media, introducing new narratives, styles, and perspectives.

American Arts

Canadian contributions to the arts, including music, visual arts, theater, and film, would become increasingly integrated into the American mainstream. Canadian musicians such as Leonard Cohen, Drake, and The Weeknd, already internationally recognized, could take on a more prominent role in shaping the American music industry. Similarly, Canadian visual artists, from painters like Emily Carr to contemporary figures like Jeff Wall could bring new techniques and perspectives to American galleries, influencing American art in profound ways.

However, the influx of Canadian talent could also spark debates about artistic originality and the blending of national styles. Would the presence of Canadian artists enrich American culture, or would it blur the lines between what constitutes American versus Canadian art? The collaboration between Canadian and American artists might result in an era of creative innovation, blending Canadian regionalism with American popular culture, potentially leading to new genres and forms of artistic expression.

In a U.S. dominated cultural landscape, Canadian literature might become more mainstream, but it could also lose some of its distinctiveness. Would Canadian authors continue to explore the themes of Canadian nationalism and multiculturalism, or would the broader American political context lead them to focus more on universal themes, aligning more closely with American literary traditions? Furthermore, American literature might incorporate more Canadian characters, settings, and historical contexts, leading to a broader, more inclusive North American literary canon.

In television and film, Canadian directors, actors, and producers would have more access to American studios, potentially leading to increased cross border collaborations. Canadian filmmakers like David Cronenberg and Xavier

Dolan could see their work reach larger American audiences, while American filmmakers might increasingly set their sights on Canadian locations for their projects. However, as American entertainment conglomerates gain more influence over the Canadian media market, Canadian filmmakers might struggle to retain their cultural autonomy.

Additionally, the language divide could complicate the integration of Canadian media into the broader American system. Canada's bilingualism, English and French, might require new approaches to media production, marketing, and distribution, particularly in regions where French is not widely spoken. Would the U.S. embrace Canada's French speaking population, or would the dominance of English language media reduce the space for French language content?

The Implications for American Identity and National Pride

The most profound impact of Canada's integration into the United States would be the reshaping of American identity. For centuries, American national pride has been deeply intertwined with the idea of the U.S. as an exceptional, independent nation with a unique place in the world. This pride has been fueled by the country's distinct political system, its role as a global superpower, and its singular cultural narrative. The integration of a neighboring, independent country like Canada would challenge these notions of singularity and exceptionalism.

On one hand, Canadians would bring with them a unique set of values and ideals, particularly related to social welfare, healthcare, multiculturalism, and bilingualism. These values might influence U.S. policy and political discourse, especially in terms of healthcare reform, immigrant integration, and language policies. The integration of Canada could encourage a more inclusive, outward-facing sense of American identity, one that embraces the diversity of North America and the shared historical and cultural connections between the two countries.

On the other hand, there could be resistance from those who fear that Canadian values might dilute the core tenets of American exceptionalism. American nationalism has often been defined by the belief in American superiority and uniqueness. The arrival of Canada, with its social policies, cultural diversity, and comparatively smaller global influence, might be viewed by some as a challenge to this long held narrative. The "melting pot" vision of America might be replaced with a more complex identity, where the distinctions between American and Canadian cultures become more pronounced, and Americans must grapple with the idea of being one part of a larger, continental entity.

National pride might also shift as Americans reframe their relationship with Canada. Americans have historically seen their neighbors to the north as a friendly but secondary player on the global stage. With Canada now a state, the lines between the two countries would be redrawn, and Americans might need to recalibrate their sense of superiority, particularly when it comes to their economic and military might. Could the U.S. accept a greater sense of shared governance, or would tensions arise over the perceived loss of control?

Finally, the question of how American identity would adapt to the introduction of French speaking Canadians and how that would impact America's language policies and cultural attitudes toward bilingualism is worth considering. Would bilingualism be embraced as a cornerstone of American identity, or would it remain a divisive issue?

A New Chapter for American Culture

If Canada were to become the 51st state, American culture would be irreversibly changed. The infusion of Canadian values, history, art, and identity would reshape the way Americans see themselves and their place in the world.

Whether this cultural shift would lead to a more inclusive, diverse North American identity or spark a reimagining of American exceptionalism depends largely on how both Canadians and Americans choose to navigate the new cultural and political realities. The union could result in a richer, more complex cultural tapestry, or it could raise profound questions about the boundaries of national pride and the meaning of American identity. The outcome would be a negotiation between old and new, familiar and foreign could define the future of American culture in a united North America.

Chapter 14
The Economic Implications

The economic implications of Canada joining the United States as its 51st state would be far-reaching and likely, positively transformative. The inclusion of an entire country with a well-developed economy, natural resources, and a unique geopolitical position would reshape both the Canadian and American economic landscapes in profound ways. From trade and investment flows to changes in economic policy and standard of living, the integration of Canada into the U.S. would have ripple effects across North America and beyond.

In this chapter, we will examine the potential economic consequences of Canada's accession to the United States, discussing changes to trade, investment, and economic policy, as well as the broader impact on the standard of living and economic growth for both Canadians and Americans.

The Economic Integration of Canada into the United States: A Major Shift

The integration of Canada into the United States would create the world's largest single economic bloc, combining the combined economic strength of two advanced economies. As of recent years, Canada's economy is the 10th largest in the world, with significant natural resources, a high standard of living, and a skilled labor force. However, as part of the United States, Canada would not only contribute these strengths but also face new economic realities that come with full membership in a much larger and more complex system.

Increased Economic Scale

The addition of Canada would significantly increase the economic scale of the United States. The U.S. economy, which currently holds a GDP of over $26 trillion, would expand with the inclusion of Canada's $2.2 trillion GDP, further solidifying the United States' position as the world's largest economy. This expansion would increase the size of the domestic market for goods and services, allowing for greater economies of scale and efficiency in production, distribution, and consumption.

While this could lead to enhanced growth opportunities for U.S. companies, it could also result in the centralization of economic power in major financial centers like New York, San Francisco, and Chicago. Canada's regional economic diversity, including its natural resource sectors in the west and technology hubs in Toronto and Montreal, could become integral parts of this larger economic system, contributing to more robust national growth across a wider range of industries.

Labor Market Adjustments

One of the key challenges would be the integration of the labor markets. Canada's workforce is highly skilled and educated, with high levels of literacy and a strong service sector, particularly in finance, technology, and healthcare. As Canadian workers were integrated into the U.S. labor market, there would likely be job displacements and sectoral shifts. Workers from traditionally strong Canadian industries like natural resource extraction, manufacturing, and public services might face challenges in adapting to the more competitive U.S. job market, particularly in areas like healthcare, social services, and unionized labor. Conversely, Canada's skilled workforce would also find more opportunities in the U.S., where sectors like technology, finance, and innovation could benefit from the influx of new talent.

Regional Disparities

While the economic benefits of a larger, unified market could be significant, regional disparities might increase. Canada's provinces and territories, with their different economies and levels of industrial development, could see varying benefits from integration. For instance, regions in central and eastern Canada that are more reliant on industries like manufacturing, transportation, and services could benefit greatly from larger access to the U.S. market. On the other hand, resource dependent provinces like Alberta, which has a robust oil and gas industry, might experience economic shifts as U.S. energy policies and environmental regulations evolve.

Furthermore, provinces with a higher cost of living, such as British Columbia and Ontario, might face increased pressure as American businesses and populations flood into these areas, potentially raising housing prices, wages, and living costs. This could widen the economic divide between different regions of the former Canada and those of the U.S.

Changes to Trade, Investment, and Economic Policy

Canada's integration into the United States would lead to significant changes in trade relations, investment flows, and economic policy.

Trade Integration and Tariff Elimination

The most immediate change would likely be the elimination of international borders for trade. Canada and the U.S. already have strong economic ties through agreements like the United States-Mexico-Canada Agreement (USMCA), but full statehood would eliminate any remaining trade barriers between the two countries. With no tariffs or trade restrictions, goods and services would move freely across the former Canada-U.S. border, resulting in cost savings, increased efficiency, and more competitive industries on both sides.

Canada's natural resources, particularly oil, gas, minerals, and forestry products, would benefit from unencumbered access to the American market, potentially strengthening the energy sector in North America. Conversely, U.S. exports of manufactured goods, electronics, and agricultural products could reach Canadian consumers without restriction, benefiting American businesses.

However, trade integration could also bring challenges. For instance, Canadian industries that rely heavily on U.S. protectionist policies or subsidies might see these supports reduced, as the U.S. government sets new economic priorities. Canada's agricultural and dairy industries, for example, which have long been protected by tariff walls, would likely face greater competition from U.S. producers.

Foreign Investment and Capital Flows

The unification of Canada and the U.S. would also change the flow of foreign investment. As one economic unit, North America would become an even more attractive destination for global investors, particularly as Canada's vast resources, skilled workforce, and trade relationships are integrated into the U.S. economic system. American firms may be more willing to invest in Canadian projects and companies, particularly in sectors like energy, technology, and infrastructure.

At the same time, there could be concerns about the potential for the U.S. to dominate the capital flows, particularly if American financial institutions increase their presence in Canadian markets. Canada's independent financial sector might struggle to retain its autonomy, as U.S.

based banks and investment firms could consolidate their dominance in the North American financial system.

Additionally, the potential for greater cross border investment might accelerate the development of joint ventures, research and development partnerships, and large-scale infrastructure projects spanning both countries.

Economic Policy Changes

With Canada becoming the 51st state, Canadian economic policies would be fully integrated into U.S. federal policy. This would have significant implications for fiscal policy, taxation, social spending, and trade regulations. Canada's social programs such as universal healthcare and a more robust social safety net could come under scrutiny as American policymakers adjust to the reality of absorbing a much more socialized system of governance.

On the U.S. side, Canada's more progressive fiscal policies might influence American debates around tax rates, social services, and government intervention. The issue of universal healthcare, in particular, could see a significant shift, as Canadians' experiences with a public health system might push the U.S. towards greater healthcare reforms.

Moreover, Canadian industries could be impacted by changes in regulatory frameworks, particularly in environmental and labor protections. Policies that were once separate would now be harmonized with U.S. standards, possibly leading to deregulation in certain sectors and more stringent regulations in others, depending on the political climate.

Impact on the Canadian and American Economy and Standard of Living

The economic effects of Canada becoming the 51st state would ripple through both the Canadian and American economies, with distinct consequences for each.

If Canada were to become the 51st state, there would be significant economic adjustments, and the Canadian dollar's exchange rate with the U.S. dollar would likely be one of the first issues to address. However, predicting exact outcomes like the Canadian dollar being traded at par with the U.S. dollar, or Canadians becoming 30-40% wealthier by having the lower valued Canadian dollar traded at par with is more valuable American counterpart, would be speculative and will depend on a range of complex factors. Let's break down the possibilities:

Canadian Dollar and U.S. Dollar Parity

Upon Canada joining the U.S., the Canadian dollar (CAD) would likely either be phased out or merged into the U.S. dollar (USD). There are a few possible scenarios.

Adoption of the U.S. Dollar

One of the most straightforward outcomes would be Canada adopting the U.S. dollar as its official currency, similar to how some countries like Panama and El Salvador use the USD. In this case, the exchange rate would no longer be a factor, as Canadians would simply use U.S. currency. This could stabilize the Canadian economy but would also mean losing the ability to control monetary policy such as interest rates or inflation through a Canadian central bank.

Maintaining a Separate Currency

If Canada decided to keep the Canadian dollar alongside the U.S. dollar, there would be significant pressure on the Canadian dollar's value. The U.S. dollar would likely become dominant, and the Canadian dollar could experience significant fluctuations depending on market perceptions of Canada's new role within the U.S. economy.

Currency Pegging

Another possibility would be Canada pegging its currency to the U.S. dollar similar to how some countries peg their currencies to the U.S. dollar today. This could stabilize the exchange rate but might come with challenges in balancing Canada's economic needs against U.S. monetary policy.

Would Canadians Become 30-40% Wealthier if their currency is pegged at par with the U.S.?

The idea that Canadians would become 30-40% wealthier if they joined the U.S. is a theoretical estimation, but it is far from certain. Here are a few considerations:

Economic Convergence

If Canada became a state, it would benefit from deeper integration into the U.S. economy, including access to larger markets, infrastructure, and investment. Over time, Canadian businesses and individuals might see increased wealth through greater economic opportunities. However, the extent to which Canadians would directly see their wealth increase would depend on factors such as wage parity, access to U.S. social benefits, and the structural changes to the Canadian economy under U.S. governance.

Increased Inequality

On the flip side, wealth distribution might also shift, with some sectors of the population potentially losing out in a transition to U.S. policies. Certain regions or industries that were previously supported by Canadian federal programs or protectionist policies might face challenges. For instance, industries like Canadian agriculture, energy, or healthcare might undergo significant transformations.

Currency Devaluation or Strengthening

If the Canadian dollar were to be replaced by the U.S. dollar or pegged at par, Canadians might experience a sharp increase in purchasing power initially, therefore, increasing their wealth by a hefty 30-40%. However, the loss of Canadian sovereignty over economic policies and the potential for inflation or market adjustments could counterbalance these gains.

In short, while there may be initial benefits from joining the U.S. in terms of access to a larger economy, infrastructure, and job markets, the overall impact on wealth distribution would depend on various factors, including the transition's social, political, and economic elements.

Long-term Impact on Wealth; Job Opportunities and Wages

Canadians might see better job opportunities in a broader U.S. labor market, especially in sectors like technology, finance, and trade. This could boost average wages in the long term, but it could also mean increased competition and regional disparities in wealth.

Social and Public Services

Canada's highly regarded social services, including universal healthcare, would likely undergo significant changes under the U.S. system. The U.S. healthcare system, for instance, is far more privatized and less accessible in terms of affordability than Canada's. This could mean Canadians losing access to some of the benefits they enjoyed under the Canadian system.

Political and Economic Adjustment Costs

The shift would not be without economic costs, including the integration of laws, taxes, and political systems. For Canadians, these adjustments could include higher costs of living in some areas, changes to social safety nets, and new economic pressures. Over time, the cost of living could increase or stabilize depending on how U.S. policies are implemented at the state level.

While the idea of Canadians becoming significantly wealthier following statehood is an interesting one, the reality would likely be far more complex. The Canadian dollar's relationship with the U.S. dollar would certainly undergo major changes, and the benefits of a larger, integrated economy would need to be weighed against the challenges of losing sovereignty and adapting to a new political and economic system. The idea of Canadians becoming wealthier if their dollar is pegged at par is speculative and would depend on many factors, including the precise manner in which the union would be carried out and how both Canadian and U.S. governments manage the transition.

Impact on the Canadian Economy

In the short term, Canada's integration into the United States could bring economic disruption, particularly in sectors that were previously protected by Canadian laws and regulations. Industries like dairy, agriculture, and telecommunications, which were shielded from American competition, would likely face a more competitive environment. While this might stimulate growth and productivity in some sectors, it could also lead to job losses in others as industries adjust to the larger American economic system.

The Canadian government's shift from an independent fiscal policy to one under the U.S. would lead to changes in taxation, public spending, and debt management. The Canadian dollar would likely be replaced by the U.S. dollar, eliminating exchange rate risks and potentially leading to price adjustments in goods and services. However, the integration process might also result in certain dislocations, particularly as Canadian industries find themselves competing with larger American firms that benefit from economies of scale.

In the long term, Canadians could benefit from a higher standard of living due to better access to U.S. markets, investment, and infrastructure. The U.S. welfare system, however, might not provide the same level of social protections and services that Canadians are accustomed to, particularly in healthcare and unemployment benefits, raising questions about the level of benefits that Canadians would lose in the transition. In return however, Canadians may actually benefit from lower tax rates and tax costs.

Impact on the American Economy

For the U.S., the economic benefits of adding Canada would be significant. Access to Canada's natural resources, including energy, forestry, and minerals, would ensure a more secure supply of key inputs to American manufacturing, infrastructure, and technology industries. The larger labor pool would also stimulate innovation, particularly in sectors like technology, finance, and green energy.

The U.S. might also experience a rise in productivity and lower prices for goods that were previously subject to tariffs or other barriers. Canadian firms would have greater access to U.S. capital and labor markets, which could fuel new industries and boost economic growth across both countries. Additionally, Canada's relatively high standard of education and skilled labor force would complement the existing U.S. workforce, enhancing the overall competitiveness of the North American region.

However, regional economic disparities might widen, especially as urban centers on both sides of the border experience increased migration and investment. Housing prices, wage inequality, and cost-of-living differences could rise in certain areas as the economic consolidation accelerates.

Impact on the Standard of Living
The integration of Canada into the U.S. would have a mixed effect on the standard of living in both countries. On one hand, the expanded access to resources, goods, and services would likely lead to higher economic growth and lower consumer prices. On the other hand, the loss of certain social programs in Canada and the increased competition for jobs could create challenges for those in lower income brackets or in regions with weaker economies.

For Canadians, the impact on healthcare and social services could be particularly pronounced. However, tax costs would likely be much lower. With the U.S. healthcare system differing significantly from Canada's public model, many Canadians might see a decline in access to affordable healthcare, which could affect overall well-being. However, the larger, unified North American economy might bring new economic opportunities, higher wages in some sectors, and a more dynamic job market.

In the U.S., the integration of Canada could bring economic benefits to many households, particularly in urban and technology-driven industries, but also risks raising costs in areas like housing and healthcare as demand increases in high-growth regions.

A Unified Economic Future

Canada's accession to the United States as the 51st state would dramatically reshape both Canadian and American economies, creating opportunities and challenges on both sides. The integration of two large, advanced economies would produce a unified North American market with enhanced economic power, but the changes in trade, investment, and economic policy would require significant adjustments. While economic growth and efficiency could rise, the disruption to labor markets, regional disparities, and the loss of social programs in Canada could present challenges. Ultimately, the standard of living in both countries could rise, but the long-term effects would depend on how governments, businesses, and workers adjust to the realities of a new, united economic system.

Impact on the Value of the Canadian Dollar if Canada Becomes the 51st State

If Canada were to become the 51st state of the United States, one of the most significant economic consequences would be the fate of the Canadian dollar (CAD). The Canadian currency, as a symbol of the country's economic autonomy and political sovereignty, would no longer have a role in a unified North American economy. The integration of Canada into the United States would likely lead to the dissolution of the Canadian dollar and its replacement with the U.S. dollar (USD), creating profound shifts in the financial landscape of Canada and the broader North American economy.

In this section, we will explore the likely impact of such a transition on the value of the Canadian dollar, considering the implications for both the exchange rate and Canada's economy as a whole.

The Likely Replacement of the Canadian Dollar with the U.S. Dollar

The most immediate and inevitable effect of Canada becoming the 51st state would be the elimination of the Canadian dollar as the nation's official currency. The U.S. dollar would likely become the sole currency for the newly expanded U.S., including both Canada and the United States. This transition would have several key implications for the value of the Canadian dollar.

Dissolution of the Canadian Dollar

The Canadian dollar, which is currently pegged to market forces and is influenced by factors like oil prices, interest rates, and Canadian fiscal policies, would no longer have any independent value in global markets. As Canada's political status shifts to that of a U.S. state, the Canadian dollar would likely be phased out. This process could take time, as the U.S. would need to exchange all Canadian banknotes and coins for U.S. dollars, and establish a system to account for all deposits, loans, and investments that were previously denominated in Canadian dollars. However, in the transition period, the Canadian dollar would likely become highly volatile, with businesses, banks, and individuals scrambling to exchange their holdings into U.S. dollars.

Exchange Rates and Currency Markets

In the period leading up to the official adoption of the U.S. dollar, the Canadian dollar would experience extreme fluctuations in value. Investors and foreign exchange markets would quickly adjust their expectations, possibly leading to a sharp devaluation of the Canadian dollar as the demand for CAD evaporates. The Canadian dollar could initially depreciate significantly against the U.S. dollar, as the market anticipates the end of its role as a separate currency.

As a result, the CAD might lose its value compared to the USD even before full implementation. Afterward, the Canadian dollar would effectively cease to exist, and the U.S. dollar would replace it in all financial transactions, including domestic trade, savings, investments, and wages.

Economic and Psychological Impacts on the Canadian Economy

The replacement of the Canadian dollar with the U.S. dollar would have immediate and long-term implications for the Canadian economy. These consequences would not only affect the value of the currency but also the broader financial and economic environment in Canada.

Impacts on Canadian Consumers and Businesses

For Canadian consumers and businesses, the transition to the U.S. dollar could potentially have both positive and negative effects. On one hand, the U.S. dollar is more stable and widely accepted internationally, which could make travel, international trade, and investments simpler. Businesses that already operate cross border, like Canadian exporters or U.S. based firms with Canadian subsidiaries would no longer need to deal with the complexities of exchange rates when trading or investing between the two countries.

However, the transition could also have negative consequences. Canadian goods and services could experience price hikes in the short term as businesses adjust to the U.S. dollar. The cost of imports, especially those coming from outside North America, might increase if exchange rates shift. Additionally, Canadian businesses that were previously able to benefit from a relatively weaker Canadian dollar such as in sectors like manufacturing and resource extraction, might face reduced competitiveness in global markets, as their products would now be priced in U.S. dollars.

For Canadians who hold savings, investments, or pensions denominated in Canadian dollars, the transition could erode the value of these assets, especially if the U.S. dollar is stronger than the Canadian dollar at the time of the switch. This would particularly impact retirees, savers, and anyone reliant on fixed-income assets like bonds.

Shifting Interest Rates and Inflation

Interest rates in Canada, once part of an independent Canadian economic policy, would likely align with U.S. Federal Reserve policies. The Bank of Canada, as an independent institution, would no longer have control over interest rates, and instead, Canadian monetary policy would be set in Washington, D.C. This means that Canada would be subject to U.S. interest rate decisions, which may not always align with Canadian economic conditions.

If the U.S. Federal Reserve raises interest rates to combat inflation or stimulate economic growth, Canada would be subject to the same changes, even if Canadian inflation rates or economic growth do not mirror U.S. trends. Similarly, if U.S. inflation rates were higher than those in Canada, the U.S. dollar could strengthen against the Canadian dollar before its dissolution, making goods and services more expensive for Canadians.

Impact on Canada's Trade and Foreign Investment

Canada's global trade relationships and foreign investment climate would also be significantly affected by the switch to the U.S. dollar.

Trade with Other Nations

One of the more immediate effects of adopting the U.S. dollar would be the shift in how Canada engages with the rest of the world. As the U.S. dollar is the world's primary reserve currency, it is widely used in international trade and finance. Canadian companies would benefit from easier trade with countries that already use the U.S. dollar or base their exchange rates on it. The elimination of currency risk between Canada and the U.S. would simplify cross border trade, which could be a boon for businesses in industries like energy, manufacturing, and technology.

However, countries that have historically dealt with Canada in Canadian dollars would now have to adjust to the new reality. While U.S. dollars are widely accepted globally, the sudden change in currency might cause temporary disruptions in trade agreements and require renegotiations of contracts and terms.

Foreign Direct Investment (FDI)

For foreign investors, the transition from the Canadian dollar to the U.S. dollar could simplify some aspects of

Canadian investment. The Canadian market would become more directly integrated with the U.S. economy, making it easier for foreign investors to buy into Canadian assets without needing to manage currency risk. This could potentially attract more foreign capital into Canada, especially from countries that rely on the U.S. dollar as a benchmark.

However, the disappearance of the Canadian dollar could discourage investment from countries that favor diversifying their portfolios into Canadian assets specifically because of the stability offered by the Canadian currency. The uniqueness of the Canadian dollar would no longer provide a differentiated investment opportunity, and foreign investors might shift their focus to other markets.

Psychological and Cultural Impact of Losing the Canadian Dollar

The psychological and cultural impact of Canada abandoning its national currency in favor of the U.S. dollar should not be underestimated. The Canadian dollar is a symbol of Canadian identity, representing the country's autonomy, sovereignty, and economic independence. The transition to the U.S. dollar could have deep cultural consequences, particularly among Canadians who value the country's distinctiveness.

In addition to economic implications, the loss of the Canadian dollar could be seen as a symbol of diminished national identity, as Canadians would no longer have their own money to represent them on the global stage. The psychological effect of this loss could influence consumer behavior, national pride, and political sentiments, especially if certain groups feel that Canadian sovereignty is further compromised by economic integration.

A New Economic Era for Canada

In conclusion, the economic implications of Canada becoming the 51st state would fundamentally alter the value of the Canadian dollar. As Canada transitions to the U.S. dollar, the Canadian dollar would likely lose its value and cease to exist, replaced by the stronger, more stable U.S. currency. This would create both opportunities and challenges for Canadians, as they adapt to a new economic reality characterized by greater integration with the U.S. market, but also new risks related to interest rates, inflation, and trade.

While the transition to the U.S. dollar could simplify cross border trade and investment, it would also disrupt the lives of Canadians who have long identified with the Canadian dollar as a symbol of their national identity. The long-term impact of this shift would depend on how Canadian businesses, consumers, and policymakers navigate the complex changes ahead. Ultimately, the value of the Canadian dollar would be subsumed within a larger North American economic system, with significant implications for the country's economic future and its place within the global economy.

Chapter 15
The Environmental Implications

If Canada were to become the 51st state of the United States, the environmental landscape of North America would undergo significant shifts. Both Canada and the U.S. have unique environmental challenges and regulatory frameworks, and integrating Canada into the U.S. system would undoubtedly lead to changes in policies, resource management, and conservation strategies. The union of the two nations would have profound effects on the stewardship of natural resources, ecosystems, and the broader environmental health of the continent.

In this chapter, we will examine the potential environmental implications of Canada joining the United States, focusing on changes to environmental policies and regulations, as well as the impact on natural resources and ecosystems.

The Potential Environmental Implications of Canada Becoming the 51st State

The integration of Canada into the United States would bring about several environmental changes. On the one hand, greater cooperation between Canada and the U.S. could lead to more unified, region-wide environmental policies. On the other hand, the differences in how both countries approach environmental issues could also create tension and challenges, especially as Canada's historically more progressive environmental policies may clash with the priorities of certain U.S. states.

A Unified Environmental Policy?

One of the most significant shifts would be the potential for the creation of a single, unified North American environmental policy. Canada's current environmental policies, which often focus on sustainability, conservation, and stricter pollution regulations, would likely need to align with U.S. federal policies. In some cases, this could lead to stronger environmental protection measures across the continent, particularly if U.S. federal agencies like the

Environmental Protection Agency (EPA) adopt more stringent regulations.

However, this integration could also create challenges, especially if U.S. policy leans more toward deregulation. Certain regions of the U.S. have historically been more resistant to strong environmental regulations, particularly in industries such as fossil fuel extraction, mining, and agriculture. Canada's more progressive approach, which includes policies such as carbon pricing and bans on certain types of pollution, might be compromised as U.S. federal policy might prioritize economic growth and energy independence over stringent environmental controls.

Balancing Economic Growth and Environmental Protection

Canada's integration into the U.S. would also have an impact on the balance between environmental protection and economic growth. Canada's economy, particularly in the western provinces like Alberta and British Columbia, relies heavily on natural resource extraction industries, including oil, gas, and forestry. These industries have significant environmental footprints, with concerns related to greenhouse gas emissions, habitat destruction, and water contamination.

As part of the U.S., Canada's natural resources would likely be subject to U.S. regulatory frameworks that prioritize economic growth, energy production, and job creation. This could result in a shift toward more aggressive resource extraction policies, possibly undermining Canada's efforts to reduce carbon emissions and protect sensitive ecosystems. The extraction of oil from the oil sands in Alberta, for example, could become even more pronounced under U.S. energy policies, potentially leading to greater environmental degradation, especially if U.S. policies are less stringent than Canada's current regulations.

Changes to Environmental Policy and Regulation

The environmental regulatory frameworks of Canada and the U.S. differ significantly, and the transition to a unified federal system would bring with it changes to the way environmental issues are governed. The Canadian federal government has historically maintained more stringent environmental laws in some areas, such as emissions reductions, climate change mitigation, and biodiversity conservation. The U.S., on the other hand, has a more varied and fragmented approach to environmental policy, with states often exercising a significant amount of autonomy over environmental issues.

U.S. Federal Environmental Policy

Upon joining the U.S., Canada would most likely fall under the umbrella of U.S. federal environmental policies, which would likely mean greater alignment with U.S. priorities. While some positive developments could emerge, such as the potential for more cohesive regional policies, the environmental agenda in the U.S. could shift based on political leadership at the federal level.

For example, the U.S. has oscillated between strong and weak environmental policies depending on the party in power. Under the Trump administration, many environmental regulations were rolled back, and priorities such as clean energy investments were deprioritized in favor of boosting fossil fuel production. Conversely, under the Biden administration, there has been a renewed focus on climate change and sustainability, with significant investments in green energy. If Canada were to join the U.S., its environmental policies could be swayed by these national shifts in political power, potentially diminishing Canada's autonomy in setting its own regulatory standards.

Harmonizing Canadian and U.S. Environmental Laws

While Canada and the U.S. already collaborate on several environmental issues, including water quality, air pollution, and wildlife conservation, the legal and regulatory differences between the two countries would require significant harmonization. For instance, Canada's environmental laws around land use, forestry, and natural resource extraction are often more robust, with a stronger emphasis on protecting biodiversity and ensuring sustainability. In the U.S., these regulations vary widely between states, and more aggressive resource extraction policies often have less stringent environmental standards.

Canada's stringent carbon pricing mechanisms and emissions reduction targets might be compromised as the U.S. focuses on economic recovery and job creation. Canada's commitment to reducing carbon emissions and transitioning to renewable energy sources could be diluted if U.S. federal policies are less focused on climate change. This might slow Canada's progress toward meeting its climate targets, undermining the significant investments Canada has made in green energy and carbon neutral technologies.

Transboundary Environmental Challenges

A significant issue in environmental policy would be the management of shared ecosystems and transboundary environmental challenges. For example, Canada and the U.S. share vast river systems such as the Great Lakes, the Columbia River, and the Mackenzie River, as well as mountain ranges like the Rocky Mountains. The management of these water bodies and ecosystems would require extensive coordination between the two countries at the federal, state, and provincial levels.

The integration of Canada into the U.S. would necessitate new governance structures to ensure that shared resources are managed sustainably. U.S. federal policies could need to address Canada's unique environmental needs, particularly in the areas of freshwater management, forest conservation, and wildlife protection. Additionally, Canada's large northern territories, home to fragile ecosystems, could see more rapid development under U.S. policies that prioritize resource extraction and energy development, potentially putting pressure on delicate habitats that have been historically protected by Canadian policies.

Impact on Canada's and America's Natural Resources and Ecosystems

The natural resources and ecosystems of both Canada and the U.S. would undergo significant changes in a unified North America, as resource management policies are restructured and re-prioritized.

Canada's Natural Resources

Canada is home to vast natural resources, including oil, gas, timber, freshwater, and minerals. The oil sands in Alberta are one of the largest known oil reserves in the world, and Canada is also a major exporter of timber, potash, and other minerals. The integration of Canada into the U.S. would likely lead to increased demand for these resources, as U.S. industries and consumers would benefit from easier access to Canadian energy and raw materials. While this could result in economic benefits for Canada, the environmental consequences of increased extraction could be significant.

Canada's oil sands are particularly controversial due to their high carbon emissions and potential to contribute to climate change. Under U.S. policies, resource extraction in Canada may intensify, especially if the U.S. prioritizes energy independence and seeks to capitalize on Canada's reserves. This could lead to an increased environmental footprint in Canada, especially in areas like Alberta, where oil sands development has already caused significant environmental damage, including deforestation, water contamination, and the disruption of Indigenous land.

Biodiversity and Conservation

Canada's natural landscapes, from the boreal forests of the north to the temperate rainforests of British Columbia, are home to some of the world's most pristine ecosystems. These areas support a wide variety of species, including bears, wolves, caribou, and migratory birds. As Canada integrates into the U.S., these ecosystems could face new pressures, as economic interests in resource extraction and land development increase.

For instance, U.S. policies that encourage land development for agriculture, logging, or urban expansion could threaten Canada's biodiversity if conservation efforts are weakened. Canada has been a global leader in the protection of biodiversity, with policies that have prioritized the creation of national parks, wildlife corridors, and the conservation of critical habitats. Under U.S. policies, there could be a greater emphasis on balancing conservation with economic development, potentially leading to compromises that may reduce the effectiveness of Canada's conservation efforts.

Impact on U.S. Natural Resources

In the U.S., the environmental implications of integrating Canada's vast natural resources could also be significant. The U.S. would gain access to Canada's freshwater resources, which are among the largest and cleanest in the world. This could lead to both economic opportunities and environmental challenges, especially in areas where water scarcity is a concern. The integration of Canada's natural resources into the U.S. economy could strain already depleted resources in regions like the western U.S., where water shortages are an ongoing issue.

Similarly, U.S. ecosystems could face new pressures from increased development and resource extraction, especially in areas of Canada that were previously protected from intensive development. The protection of U.S. ecosystems might require additional federal regulation to prevent further environmental degradation.

A Complex Environmental Landscape

The environmental implications of Canada becoming the 51st state are complex. While there is potential for more unified environmental policies and increased cooperation between Canada and the U.S., the risks of weakened environmental protections are significant. Canada's traditionally more progressive environmental policies, particularly in resource management, conservation, and climate change, could be diluted as U.S. policies shift toward economic growth and energy independence.

The impact on Canada's natural resources, especially oil, gas, and forestry, could be profound, with increased demand for these resources potentially resulting in greater environmental degradation. Similarly, the loss of Canadian control over its ecosystems could weaken efforts to protect biodiversity, particularly in vulnerable areas like the boreal forests and northern tundra.

Ultimately, the environmental implications of Canada joining the U.S. would depend on the degree to which both countries could reconcile their differences in environmental priorities and find ways to protect shared ecosystems while allowing for economic growth. Integration could require careful negotiation and adaptation to ensure that both countries' natural resources are managed sustainably for future generations.

Chapter 16
The Impact on Canadian Foreign Policy

The hypothetical scenario of Canada becoming the 51st state of the United States would have far-reaching consequences not only on the domestic politics and economy of both nations but also on their roles in the global arena. One of the most profound areas of transformation would be in foreign policy. As an independent nation, Canada has pursued its own foreign policy for decades, fostering diplomatic relations and pursuing international goals that sometimes differ from those of the U.S. With the merger of the two countries, Canada would no longer operate as an autonomous entity on the world stage. Its foreign policy would likely be subsumed under U.S. leadership, creating new dynamics in both North American relations and global diplomacy.

In this chapter, we will examine the potential impact of Canada's integration into the U.S. on both countries' foreign policy, the resulting changes in relationships with other nations, and the broader implications for their roles in international affairs.

The Impact of Union on Canadian and American Foreign Policy

Upon Canada becoming the 51st state, the foreign policy landscape for both countries would be greatly altered. Currently, Canada and the U.S. share a close and often cooperative foreign policy relationship. However, as separate entities, each country has its own diplomatic priorities, international alliances, and global objectives. The integration of Canada into the U.S. would lead to several important shifts in how both countries conduct foreign affairs.

Loss of Independent Canadian Foreign Policy

As the 51st state, Canada could lose its ability to formulate an independent foreign policy. Canadian diplomatic representation, currently centered in embassies and consulates around the world, would likely be absorbed into the U.S. State Department. Canadian policymakers would no longer have the option to choose representatives to foreign policy offices, as decisions would be made at the federal level in Washington, D.C.

Canada's longstanding foreign policy values, such as a strong commitment to peacekeeping, multilateralism, and human rights would likely become less pronounced in favor of U.S. centric priorities. For instance, Canada's leadership in international peacekeeping missions, such as its involvement in UN peacekeeping operations, could be subordinated to U.S. interests, which may not prioritize such efforts. Moreover, Canada's long-standing emphasis on diplomacy and non-intervention could give way to more aggressive foreign policy stances if the U.S. moves toward military interventionism, as it has at times in recent decades.

Consolidation of Military and Defense Policy
Canada's military and defense policy would also probably shift dramatically under the U.S. security umbrella. As a member of NATO and NORAD, Canada currently cooperates with the U.S. on defense matters, but Canada maintains its own military structure and independent defense strategies. As the 51st state, Canada would no longer have an independent military force. The U.S. Department of Defense would likely oversee Canadian defense policy, potentially leading to greater alignment in defense spending, military operations, and international interventions.

Canada's role in peacekeeping or serving as a neutral actor in international disputes could diminish, as the U.S. military's focus has historically been on security, military alliances, and defense of its own geopolitical interests. This could limit Canada's ability to position itself as a neutral, peace building force in international crises.

Changes to Canada's and America's Relationships with Other Countries

The integration of Canada into the United States could fundamentally reshape how both nations relate to other countries, with consequences for diplomatic ties, trade relations, and international cooperation. While the U.S. has historically dominated international relations in the Western Hemisphere, Canada has maintained independent diplomatic relationships with other nations, often acting as a bridge between the U.S. and countries around the world.

Canada's Loss of Diplomatic Influence

Canada's international standing as an independent nation could be diminished. Countries around the world, particularly those in the Commonwealth and in Europe, view Canada as a distinct entity with its own voice in global affairs. Canada has leveraged its reputation as a peace loving, neutral country to broker negotiations and mediate conflicts. As the 51st state, Canada's diplomatic efforts would be overshadowed by the broader policies and priorities of the

U.S. As part of a superpower, Canada would no longer have the autonomy to chart its own course in international relations.

Additionally, Canada's historically close ties with the United Kingdom, France, and other Commonwealth countries could become strained, as these nations may view the merger with the U.S. as a shift away from Canada's traditional international relationships. Multilateral organizations such as the United Nations, the Commonwealth of Nations, and the Francophonie would have to adjust to the loss of a distinct Canadian voice, which could limit Canada's influence in these organizations.

Strengthened U.S.-Canada Relations with Neighbors
While Canada's foreign policy could be subsumed into the U.S., its status as the 51st state could also lead to stronger diplomatic relations between the newly unified country and its neighbors. Relations between the U.S. and Mexico, already cooperative due to NAFTA and its successor USMCA, could deepen as Canada's resources and trade ties are incorporated into the broader economic framework of North America. The continent could possibly enjoy even more integrated political, economic, and security relationships, with a shared interest in issues such as border security, migration, and trade.

Furthermore, Canada's inclusion could strengthen U.S.-Latin American relations, particularly as the newly formed North American bloc would wield increased geopolitical influence in the Western Hemisphere. The U.S. and Canada's joint efforts would likely enhance their collective influence in Latin America, both economically and diplomatically.

Shifts in Relationships with Global Powers
As part of the U.S., Canada's diplomatic leverage in international trade agreements and global governance could potentially be overshadowed by the U.S. As a member of organizations like the World Trade Organization (WTO) and the United Nations, Canada currently negotiates as an independent member. However, Canada's ability to engage in independent trade deals could be diminished, as trade negotiations would possibly be led by U.S. policymakers.

This shift could also impact Canada's relationship with emerging global powers such as China, India, and Russia. Canada has developed its own foreign policy approach to these nations, often emphasizing diplomatic engagement, trade, and conflict resolution. As part of the U.S., Canada would likely fall under U.S. foreign policy in these regions, which could be more confrontational or aligned with specific economic interests. Canada's role as a neutral broker in international disputes could diminish, particularly in sensitive areas such as international trade, human rights, and climate change negotiations.

Implications for Canada's and America's Role in International Affairs

Canada and the U.S. currently maintain prominent roles in international organizations, global security, and trade. However, if Canada were to become the 51st state, the geopolitical and diplomatic implications would be far reaching, changing the way both countries participate in global affairs.

Canada's Role in International Institutions

Canada has traditionally been a strong advocate for multilateralism and global cooperation, holding influential positions in international institutions like the United Nations, the World Bank, and the International Monetary Fund. As part of the U.S., Canada would possibly lose its ability to pursue independent leadership in these organizations. Canada's diplomatic voice would be absorbed into the U.S.'s broader strategies, meaning Canada would likely have less influence over decisions made in these forums.

On the other hand, the merger could strengthen the U.S.'s ability to shape global policies. As a more powerful entity, the U.S. and its newly expanded borders could have a stronger influence on international law, security, and trade. The combined diplomatic weight of the U.S. and Canada could make North America even more central in global diplomacy, but Canada's unique perspectives, such as its commitment to human rights, climate change action, and peacebuilding might be diluted.

Impact on Global Security and Peacekeeping
Canada has long been known for its role in peacekeeping missions and diplomatic mediation, often positioning itself as a neutral actor in conflicts around the world. The loss of this independent foreign policy could significantly alter the global security environment. As part of the U.S., Canada's military, foreign aid, and peacekeeping efforts would be directed by U.S. priorities, which might not always align with Canada's previous focus on diplomacy and humanitarian aid.

The shift in priorities could have serious consequences for global conflict resolution. Canada's influence in peace negotiations, particularly in volatile regions such as the Middle East and Africa, could be diminished. In the U.S. led geopolitical framework, military interventionism could take precedence over peaceful solutions, reducing the ability to act as a neutral, noncombatant peace broker.

Environmental and Climate Diplomacy

One of the areas where Canada's independent voice would be most strongly missed is in international environmental diplomacy. Canada has historically been a leader in global climate agreements, particularly through initiatives such as the Paris Agreement and its role in protecting global biodiversity. Under U.S. leadership, Canada's ability to push for progressive climate policies could be sidelined, especially if U.S. priorities shift towards economic growth over environmental protection. Canada's more aggressive carbon reduction and renewable energy initiatives could become secondary to U.S. energy policies, which are more focused on fossil fuels and energy independence.

A Shifting Landscape for Global Diplomacy

In conclusion, the impact of Canada becoming the 51st state on foreign policy would be immense, with both positive and negative ramifications. On one hand, Canada's integration into the U.S. could streamline North American diplomacy, strengthen U.S.-Canada relations, and bolster regional security. However, the loss of an independent Canadian foreign policy would undermine Canada's unique diplomatic role in the world, limiting its influence in multilateral organizations, peacekeeping efforts, and climate diplomacy.

Canada's relationships with other countries, particularly those in the Commonwealth and Europe, would likely change as its status as a sovereign nation was diminished. The broader geopolitical landscape could shift, with the U.S. assuming a greater role in international governance, leaving less room for Canada to assert its own interests. Ultimately, while the union of the two nations might increase North American influence on the global stage, it would come at the cost of Canada's distinct diplomatic voice and its ability to lead on certain global issues.

Chapter 17

The American Perspective

The prospect of Canada becoming the 51st state of the United States is a hypothetical scenario that would deeply reshape the geopolitical landscape of North America. While the notion of Canadian integration into the U.S. might seem improbable to many, the potential implications of such a union are worth exploring. From an American perspective, Canada's accession would have profound consequences on various aspects of American society, economy, and international relations.

In this chapter, we will examine the potential impact of Canada becoming the 51st state from an American viewpoint, exploring both the benefits and drawbacks for the United States.

Additionally, we will delve into the possible implications for American foreign policy and national security, considering how the U.S. might respond to the integration of its northern neighbor and the resulting shifts in global influence.

The Potential Impact of Canada Becoming the 51st State from an American Perspective

From an American standpoint, the addition of Canada as the 51st state could represent both an opportunity and a challenge. The integration of a large, resource rich nation with a highly developed economy, robust political institutions, and a distinct cultural identity would undoubtedly present a series of benefits and complications.

A Larger, Stronger Nation

First and foremost, the United States could expand geographically, gaining a vast amount of land, natural resources, and a significant population increase. Canada is the second largest country in the world by land area, and its integration would extend the U.S. borders from the Atlantic to the Pacific Ocean, including vast northern territories. This landmass would significantly increase the U.S.'s control over

North American geography, offering expanded economic, military, and environmental advantages.

Canada's vast natural resources, including oil, natural gas, minerals, and timber, would become available to the U.S. more directly. Canada is one of the world's largest energy producers, and its oil sands in Alberta are among the largest oil reserves globally. Access to these resources could bolster the U.S. energy sector, potentially reducing dependence on foreign oil imports. Moreover, Canada's freshwater resources, particularly from the Great Lakes and other northern sources, would become even more strategically important as global water scarcity becomes an increasingly pressing issue.

Economic Integration

The addition of Canada to the U.S. would also mean the full integration of the Canadian economy into the American economic system. While the two countries already enjoy one of the world's largest and most integrated trading relationships, with Canada being the U.S.'s largest trading partner, the union would simplify trade, eliminate tariffs, and harmonize economic policies across North America.

A major economic benefit would be the elimination of barriers to cross border trade, making it easier for businesses and workers to move between the U.S. and Canada. U.S. companies would gain access to Canadian markets without facing the regulatory or tariff barriers that currently exist between the two countries. This integration could create greater economic synergy, particularly in industries like manufacturing, technology, and agriculture.

Moreover, Canada's highly educated workforce, which consistently ranks among the world's best, would be a valuable addition to the American labor force. Canadian professionals, engineers, scientists, and business leaders would contribute further to U.S. innovation and productivity.

Potential Benefits and Drawbacks for the United States

While the addition of Canada to the U.S. could bring many potential benefits, there are also a number of challenges and drawbacks that would need to be considered. From an economic, political, and cultural perspective, the union would be a complex process requiring significant adjustments on all sides.

Benefits of Canadian Integration Strategic Natural Resources

One of the key advantages for the U.S. would be gaining access to Canada's wealth of natural resources. The U.S. could benefit from Canadian oil, gas, minerals, and timber supplies, which would further solidify its position as a dominant player in global energy markets. The incorporation of Canada's vast freshwater reserves would also provide the U.S. with a critical resource in an increasingly water scarce world.

Economic Growth and Market Expansion

Canada's highly developed economy would boost the size of the U.S. economy, creating a more powerful North American economic bloc. By removing trade barriers and harmonizing economic policies, both nations would likely experience faster growth, increased efficiency, and greater competitiveness in the global market.

Cultural and Technological Synergies

The U.S. and Canada share many cultural, social, and technological ties, and their integration would deepen these connections. Canada's technological innovations, particularly in sectors like clean energy, artificial intelligence, and telecommunications, would benefit the U.S., fostering greater innovation and the development of cutting-edge industries.

Political and Military Power

A unified North America would exert an even greater influence on global politics and security. With Canada's strong political institutions and stable democracy, the U.S. would gain a more powerful ally in international affairs. Canada's integration could also strengthen U.S. defense capabilities, as the two countries share the world's longest undefended border and are already key partners in NORAD, the North American Aerospace Defense Command. The U.S. could benefit from even greater control over its northern borders and enhanced coordination on matters of national security.

Political and Administrative Challenges

Integrating a new country with a different political and legal system could pose significant challenges. Canada's political system, which includes a parliamentary government, differs from the U.S. presidential system, and harmonizing these systems would require extensive reforms. Furthermore, Canada's legal framework and its commitment to bilingualism would likely necessitate adjustments at the federal level, creating potential friction.

Cultural Tensions

While Canada and the U.S. share many cultural similarities, the two nations are distinct in certain key areas. Canada has a unique identity, shaped by its history, its relationship with Indigenous populations, its bilingualism, and its distinct social policies, such as universal healthcare. Many Canadians take pride in their country's identity as a middle power and a peacekeeping nation, and there could be resistance to being fully integrated into the U.S. system. U.S. citizens, in turn, may see this integration as a challenge to their own cultural values, particularly in regions where political differences are more pronounced.

Economic Disparities

While Canada's economy is strong, it is still smaller than that of the United States. The integration of a smaller economy into a much larger one could create imbalances in wealth distribution and lead to regional disparities. While the U.S. would benefit from access to Canada's resources, Canadian provinces with less economic output might face challenges adjusting to the U.S. economic system, particularly in sectors like agriculture, manufacturing, and natural resource extraction.

Costs of Integration

Incorporating Canada into the U.S. would also come with substantial financial and administrative costs. The U.S. could need to invest heavily in integrating Canadian infrastructure, social programs, and legal systems. Moreover, the process of assimilating millions of new citizens and adjusting governance structures would likely require extensive resources and political coordination.

Implications for American Foreign Policy and National Security

The integration of Canada into the U.S. would have significant implications for American foreign policy and national security. As a unified nation, the U.S. and Canada would become a much more powerful force in international politics. However, this newfound power would require careful management, particularly in terms of diplomacy and military engagement.

Unified Foreign Policy

With Canada as a part of the U.S., there would be a single, unified foreign policy governing North American relations.

This could streamline diplomatic efforts, particularly with countries in the Western Hemisphere. For instance, the U.S. and Canada could work more closely together on issues such as trade, migration, and security. The U.S. would likely consolidate its influence in Latin America, using the combined resources and diplomatic weight of the two countries to shape economic and political outcomes across the region.

However, Canada's independent international relationships, especially with the United Kingdom, France, and the Commonwealth could be subsumed by U.S. priorities. Canada's unique diplomatic voice, particularly in global peacekeeping and multilateral organizations, would likely be lost, and U.S. foreign policy might dominate global negotiations.

Security and Defense

On the national security front, the merger would enhance the U.S.'s ability to defend its northern borders and coordinate security efforts with Canada. The U.S. and Canada already cooperate closely through NORAD, and the addition of Canadian military assets and infrastructure would increase U.S. military power. This could be especially important as the U.S. focuses on securing its position as the global leader in defense technology and military reach.

However, a larger, more geographically expansive country could also face increased security challenges, especially in terms of managing the vast northern territories and borders. The U.S. would need to adjust its national security strategy to incorporate Canada's unique geographic, cultural, and environmental features into its defense planning.

Global Power Dynamics

A U.S.-Canada union would increase North American influence in global politics. As the largest and most economically powerful country in the Western Hemisphere, the U.S. would further consolidate its role as the world's superpower. The union would amplify U.S. political and military strength, positioning the country as an even more formidable player in global negotiations, trade deals, and international organizations.

However, this increased influence could lead to tensions with other global powers. For instance, China, Russia, and the European Union might see the U.S.-Canada union as a strategic shift that could challenge existing global alliances and economic blocs. These countries could respond by adjusting their foreign policies to counterbalance the growing dominance of the U.S. in global affairs.

A Complex Future for the United States

From an American perspective, the integration of Canada as the 51st state presents both tremendous opportunities and significant challenges. The union would create a larger, more resource-rich nation with the potential for economic growth, stronger security, and increased global influence. However, it would also require navigating complex political, cultural, and economic hurdles.

In terms of foreign policy, the U.S. could need to balance its newfound power with the integration of Canada's diplomatic voice and interests. National security would be enhanced, but the U.S. would also need to adapt its strategies to manage the larger, more diverse geographical landscape. Ultimately, while the prospect of a unified North America holds considerable advantages for the U.S., it would require careful planning, coordination, and cooperation to ensure that both countries benefit from the union and maintain their positions as global leaders in the 21st century.

Chapter 18
The Global Implications

The potential for Canada to become the 51st state of the United States would be a transformative event, not just for the countries involved, but for the entire global order. The integration of Canada into the U.S. would redefine North American geopolitics, alter international power structures, and influence global governance. The ripple effects would be felt in international relations, diplomatic alliances, and participation in multilateral organizations such as the United Nations (UN), the World Trade Organization (WTO), and NATO. Canada's unique position on the global stage, advocating for peacekeeping, human rights, and multilateralism could be absorbed into the broader policies of the U.S., shifting the balance of global diplomacy and altering power dynamics around the world.

This chapter explores the global implications of Canada becoming the 51st state, with a focus on international relations, global governance, and the potential consequences for the United Nations and other international organizations.

The idea of Canada joining the United States would be a watershed moment in global geopolitics, fundamentally altering both countries' roles on the world stage. The U.S. would emerge as an even more dominant superpower, while Canada's influence as an independent nation would diminish. The shift in power would have profound consequences for global political, economic, and military dynamics.

Expansion of U.S. Influence

One of the most significant global implications would be the consolidation of U.S. power and influence. Canada, as the world's second-largest country by land area, would provide the U.S. with an expanded geopolitical footprint. The inclusion of Canada would further solidify U.S. dominance in the Western Hemisphere and enhance its strategic positioning on the global stage. The U.S. would become even more geographically expansive, controlling vast natural resources, including some of the world's largest oil reserves and significant freshwater sources.

The combined political, economic, and military might of the U.S. and Canada would make North America an even more powerful bloc in global affairs. The U.S. would benefit from Canada's wealth of resources, its strong technological and educational institutions, and its stable democratic system. This expansion would increase American power, particularly in the realms of culture, media, and public diplomacy, as the U.S. and Canada share many cultural similarities.

However, this consolidation of power could also provoke geopolitical tensions, particularly from global powers such as China, Russia, and the European Union, which may view this union as a challenge to the current international balance of power.

Loss of Canadian Autonomy

For Canada, becoming part of the United States would mean the loss of its independent voice in global diplomacy. Canada has long played a unique role on the world stage, emphasizing multilateralism, human rights, and peacekeeping. Its position as a middle power, a nation that fosters cooperation among global actors, would be absorbed into U.S. foreign policy, which has historically been more interventionist and focused on projecting military power.

This shift would likely diminish Canada's ability to engage as an independent actor in international organizations like the United Nations. Its role as a peacekeeping force, a leader in climate change advocacy, and a supporter of human rights initiatives could be overshadowed by U.S. priorities, which are often more pragmatic or strategically driven.

Impact on International Relations and Global Governance

The integration of Canada into the United States would ripple through international relations, affecting diplomatic ties, trade agreements, and geopolitical power dynamics. The U.S. would gain additional diplomatic clout, while Canada's distinctive voice and policies could be absorbed into broader American interests.

Diplomatic Realignments

Many countries around the world would have to adjust to the new reality of a unified North American superstate. Canada has cultivated strong bilateral relationships with numerous nations, particularly within the Commonwealth and with countries in Europe. Its diplomatic role has often been that of a mediator and neutral party, advocating for peace, security, and international cooperation. As part of the U.S., Canada could lose this independent diplomatic voice, making the U.S. the dominant actor in North American diplomacy.

Canada's historical relationships with countries like the United Kingdom, France, and other Commonwealth nations could shift, as these countries may view the merger as an erosion of Canada's separate identity. Similarly, Canada's reputation as a middle power, with a focus on diplomacy over military intervention, would be subsumed under the U.S. government's foreign policy, which has often emphasized military strength and global economic leadership.

Economic Realignment

Canada's integration into the U.S. would have significant consequences for global trade relations. As the two countries already enjoy one of the most integrated trade relationships in the world, the merger would eliminate trade barriers and result in a single economic bloc covering the entire North American continent. This could create new opportunities for international businesses but would also shift trade patterns, particularly with countries outside of North America.

The newly expanded U.S. would possess an even stronger negotiating position in international trade agreements, potentially reshaping global economic alliances. Canada's participation in multilateral trade forums like the World Trade Organization (WTO) would be absorbed into the U.S. system, which could change the dynamics of trade negotiations and potentially alter existing trade relationships with the European Union, China, and other major global players.

Shifting Global Alliances

The merger would also reshape the strategic alliances of both nations. As a larger, more powerful entity, the U.S. would have even more leverage in international diplomacy and defense, particularly within organizations like NATO, the G7, and the G20. A unified U.S.-Canada bloc could offer greater security coordination and economic cooperation within North America and extend this influence globally.

However, this increased dominance of the U.S. could strain existing relationships with other nations. Countries that previously enjoyed favorable relationships with Canada, such as those in the Global South or smaller middle powers, might feel marginalized by the more assertive foreign policy priorities of the U.S. In particular, countries that have relied on Canada's role as a peacekeeping nation might be concerned that the merged entity would be less committed to non-intervention and conflict resolution.

Implications for the United Nations and Other International Organizations

The United Nations, the World Trade Organization, NATO, and other international bodies would all be impacted by the addition of Canada to the U.S. As Canada's foreign policy voice would be subsumed into that of the U.S., the global balance of influence within these organizations would shift.

United Nations

Canada has long been an advocate for multilateralism, humanitarianism, and peacekeeping within the United Nations. The country has served as a significant contributor to UN peacekeeping missions and has been active in promoting human rights and environmental protection on the global stage. If Canada were to become the 51st state, its role within the UN would likely diminish, as its diplomatic efforts would be subsumed by the U.S., a permanent member of the UN Security Council with veto power.

The loss of Canada's independent voice would be particularly notable in international debates on peacekeeping, environmental protection, and human rights. While the U.S.

shares many of these values, its foreign policy priorities have often been more focused on security, military interventions, and economic interests. This could reduce the overall influence of the UN on key issues such as global conflict resolution, climate change, and the promotion of democratic governance.

Moreover, Canada's independent membership in UN agencies, such as the UN Human Rights Council, would be eliminated, leading to a reshaped diplomatic landscape. The U.S. would retain its dominant position, but the absence of Canada's more neutral and diplomatic approach could limit the UN's ability to broker peace and mediate international conflicts.

World Trade Organization and Global Trade

As the 51st state, Canada's status in the World Trade Organization would change. Currently, Canada negotiates trade deals as an independent member of the WTO, advocating for free trade and the reduction of trade barriers. If Canada joined the U.S., its trade negotiations would fall under U.S. jurisdiction, with the potential to shift the priorities of the WTO and trade agreements.

The merger would create an economic superstate that would possess greater leverage in global trade discussions. While this could potentially streamline trade negotiations and lead to better terms for the U.S.-Canada bloc, it could also strain existing relationships with trade partners, particularly smaller developing nations that might feel sidelined by the dominance of a larger North American trading bloc.

NATO and Global Defense

The integration of Canada into the U.S. would further solidify North American defense within NATO, the North Atlantic Treaty Organization. As members of NATO, the U.S. and Canada already collaborate closely on defense and security issues, particularly in the North Atlantic and the Arctic. The combined military resources of both countries would make North America even more dominant in terms of global security and defense capabilities.

However, this could also provoke reactions from other global powers, particularly Russia, China, and some European nations, who may view the expansion of NATO as a threat to their own spheres of influence. The growing U.S.-Canada defense partnership could contribute to an arms race or increase military tensions in key geopolitical regions.

A New Global Order

The global implications of Canada becoming the 51st state would be profound, with significant changes to international relations, global governance, and the balance of power. The U.S. would emerge as a more powerful superstate, capable of exerting greater influence in trade, security, and diplomacy. However, the merger would also mean the loss of Canada's independent voice on the world stage, potentially diminishing its role in peacekeeping, multilateralism, and human rights advocacy.

In international organizations such as the United Nations, the World Trade Organization, and NATO, the merger would shift the balance of influence, with the U.S. taking on an even more dominant role. Canada's unique contributions to global diplomacy and governance would be absorbed by U.S. priorities, altering the nature of international negotiations and cooperation.

Ultimately, the integration of Canada into the U.S. would redefine the global order, creating a more centralized North American bloc while potentially reshaping international alliances, trade relationships, and diplomatic strategies. The resulting shift in power dynamics would be felt worldwide, influencing everything from global security to economic cooperation and environmental policy for years to come.

Chapter 19
The Process of Union

The idea of Canada becoming the 51st state of the United States is a hypothetical scenario that would require a complex and unprecedented series of legal, political, and social steps. This process would not only involve the two governments but also their respective citizens, as well as international implications. Though Canada and the U.S. have shared a close relationship for centuries, the notion of full political union would require significant changes to the legal and constitutional frameworks of both countries. The potential steps involved in achieving such a union would be monumental and would need to address issues of governance, identity, and national sovereignty.

This chapter explores what the process of Canada becoming the 51st state might look like, the steps that might need to be taken, and the timeline and milestones that would accompany such an ambitious transformation.

The Potential Process of Canada Becoming the 51st State

For Canada to become the 51st state, the process would likely involve both constitutional and legislative actions in Canada, the United States, and internationally. Although no formal process currently exists for one country to join the U.S. as a state, several historical precedents from the admission of previous states may offer guidance on how such a union could unfold.

The first and most fundamental obstacle to such a union would be Canada's status as an independent nation. Canada is a sovereign state, a member of international organizations like the United Nations, and a member of the Commonwealth of Nations. Any move toward joining the United States would require the negotiation of both domestic and international agreements to dissolve Canada's sovereignty and incorporate it into the U.S. political system.

The U.S. Constitution, under Article IV, Section 3, permits the admission of new states, but the process is far from simple. Historically, new states have been admitted through an act of Congress, typically initiated after territory petitions for statehood and after a formal referendum has been held. In Canada's case, the process would begin with both domestic and international negotiations, followed by legal steps to amend both the Canadian and U.S. constitutions.

Potential Steps Involved in Achieving Union
Public Support and Political Will

The first step toward union would be securing public support for the idea of becoming the 51st state. This would require an extensive political campaign to convince both Canadians and Americans of the benefits of such a union. In Canada, the debate would likely center around issues such as national identity, economic integration, and sovereignty. In the U.S., the conversation would probably focus on economic benefits, security concerns, and how the union might affect domestic politics.

For this process to begin, a national referendum or series of regional referendums in Canada would likely be necessary. These votes would serve to gauge whether the majority of Canadians in all provinces and territories support the idea of union. Given the significant changes to Canada's political structure and identity that would result from such a move, public opinion would be crucial in determining the feasibility of union.

Agreement on Terms of Union

Once public support has been garnered, formal discussions between Canadian and U.S. governments would need to begin. These discussions would address key aspects of the union, including the terms under which Canada would join the United States. For example:

Economic Integration

Discussions would need to address issues related to currency, trade, taxation, and financial regulation. Given that Canada already has strong trade relations with the U.S., these aspects may be relatively straightforward, but they would still require the negotiation of new agreements to integrate Canada fully into the U.S. economic system.

Political Representation

The question of how Canada would be represented in the U.S. government would likely be a central issue. Canada's provinces and territories would likely be represented as states, but the exact political structure of governance would require careful negotiation. The integration of Canada's population into the U.S. electoral system and Congress would require the creation of new congressional districts and the establishment of voting rights for Canadians.

Language and Culture

Canada is officially bilingual, with French and English as its two official languages. The U.S., on the other hand, has no official language at the federal level, though English is the de facto national language. The process could require agreements to ensure the protection of the French language and cultural heritage, particularly in Quebec and other French speaking areas.

Legal and Constitutional Adjustments

Both the U.S. and Canada would need to amend their constitutions. For Canada, this would involve negotiations with each province to dismantle the country's federal system of government and dissolve its constitution. At the same time, the U.S. would need to pass legislation to allow Canada's accession, likely involving the approval of Congress and a possible amendment to the U.S. Constitution.

International and Diplomatic Considerations

Canada's transition into the U.S. would have significant implications for international relations. Canada's membership in international organizations, such as the United Nations, the World Trade Organization, and NATO, would need to be addressed. Canada would no longer be a separate member of these organizations, and its membership status would need to be absorbed into the U.S.

The process would likely involve formal discussions with other nations to secure their approval for the union. In particular, countries with longstanding diplomatic relationships with Canada, such as the United Kingdom, France, and other Commonwealth nations, would need to adjust their diplomatic ties to the new U.S.-Canada union.

Transition of Government and Institutions

Once the terms of union have been agreed upon, the practical process of transitioning Canada into the U.S. would begin. This would involve the incorporation of Canadian political institutions, legal frameworks, and government functions into the broader U.S. system.

One of the most complicated elements of this transition would be the integration of Canada's federal system of government into the U.S. presidential system. While

Canada's provinces would likely be converted into U.S. states, adjustments to the Canadian political structure would need to occur to ensure smooth governance. Additionally, Canada's legal system, which operates under the British common law tradition, would need to be harmonized with the U.S. system, which is based on federalism and the Constitution. Furthermore, the Quebec legal system is a Civil one, not Common Law as in the U.S. and the rest of Canada, which would further complicate the process of legal harmonization.

Timeline and Milestones for Union

The timeline for Canada becoming the 51st state would likely unfold over several years, perhaps even a decade or more, due to the complexity of the legal, political, and social changes required. Below is a potential timeline and possible key milestones:

Year 1-2: Political Campaign and Public Debate

Political Campaign: Proponents of union would begin a nationwide campaign in Canada to educate the public about the benefits and challenges of becoming the 51st state. This could include town halls, media campaigns, and consultations with provinces.

Public Opinion Polls and Regional Referendums: A series of regional referendums would take place to gauge public support for the union in different parts of the country. A national referendum would likely be held as well to determine whether Canada as a whole supports joining the United States.

Year 3-5: Formal Negotiations Begin

Initiation of Negotiations: If a majority of Canadians support union, formal negotiations between the Canadian and U.S. governments would begin. Key issues such as economic integration, legal harmonization, and political representation would be discussed.

International Consultations: The U.S. and Canada would begin talks with international organizations and countries, including the United Nations, the World Trade Organization, and Commonwealth nations, to address the potential implications of Canada's accession.

Year 5-7: Constitutional Amendments and Legislative Actions

Constitutional Amendments: The U.S. would pass the necessary legislation to admit Canada as the 51st state, and both the U.S. and Canadian constitutions would be amended. This would likely require the approval of Congress and a significant restructuring of Canada's federal government.

Approval of Canadian Provinces: Each of Canada's provinces would need to approve the dissolution of its separate government and agree to join the U.S. as individual states. This would require careful negotiations at the provincial level and could take several years to finalize. The greatest challenges would probably be the provinces of Quebec and Alberta.

Year 7-10: Final Transition and Integration

Integration of Political Institutions: The final stage would involve the transition of Canadian political institutions into the U.S. system. This would include the creation of new congressional districts, the integration of Canada's and Quebec's legal systems, and the establishment of voting rights for Canadians.

Cultural and Legal Transition: Efforts could possibly be made to ensure the protection of Canada's cultural heritage, including the preservation of French language rights, and the integration of Canadian laws into the U.S. system.

Official Union: After all legal, political, and economic structures are in place, Canada would formally become the 51st state of the United States, and the countries would officially begin their new relationship as one unified nation.

A Long and Complex Journey

The process of Canada becoming the 51st state of the United States would be an extraordinarily complex, multifaceted endeavor that would unfold over many years. It would require the approval of both Canadian and U.S. citizens, as well as the successful negotiation of numerous legal, political, and economic challenges. While the steps outlined here are speculative, they provide a framework for understanding the monumental scope of such a transformation.

The timeline for such a union could span several years or even decades, with key milestones along the way, including public referendums, constitutional amendments, and extensive international consultations. Ultimately, this process would be an unprecedented chapter in the history of both nations, fundamentally reshaping the future of North America and the global order.

Chapter 20
The Referendum Question

The notion of Canada becoming the 51st state of the United States is an extraordinary and highly hypothetical scenario, but it presents intriguing questions about how democratic processes would unfold in a country that values its sovereignty and national identity. One of the most critical components of this potential shift would be a national referendum, the process by which the people of Canada would decide whether or not to join the U.S. This referendum would serve as a pivotal moment in Canadian history, marking profound crossroads in the country's relationship with itself and with its neighbor to the south.

The question of whether to join the United States would require a comprehensive and carefully considered referendum, as it would involve not only the future of Canada's political structure but also its cultural identity, economic systems, and place in the international order. In this chapter, we will examine the potential role of a referendum in deciding Canada's future as part of the U.S., the implications such a referendum would have on Canadian democracy and sovereignty, and the consequences for Canadian national unity.

The Role of a Referendum in Deciding Whether Canada Should Become the 51st State

A referendum is a direct democratic process that allows citizens to vote on significant national issues. In the case of Canada's potential union with the U.S., a referendum would likely be the ultimate mechanism for deciding the fate of the country. Since the move would alter Canada's very identity, governance, and relationship with the world, a referendum could be essential in determining the legitimacy and consent of the Canadian people.

Public Engagement and Legitimacy

In any democratic system, the legitimacy of a decision regarding national identity and sovereignty depends on the extent to which it reflects the will of the people. The referendum could provide an opportunity for citizens across the country to express their opinion on the union. This would not only validate the process but also ensure that the decision was made transparently and democratically, upholding the fundamental principle of popular sovereignty.

The wording of the referendum question itself would be critical. It would need to be carefully phrased to allow voters to fully understand the implications of the choice at hand. A simple "Yes or No" question would likely be insufficient given the complexity of the issue. Instead, the referendum question might need to outline specific conditions, such as the political, economic, and social changes that would accompany union with the U.S. The public would need to be well-informed about what a union would entail in terms of governance, sovereignty, economic integration, and cultural shifts.

Provincial and Territorial Participation

Canada is a diverse country, with distinct regions, languages, and cultures. The question of union with the U.S. would likely be decided by referendum at both the national level and the provincial or territorial level. Given the deep political, economic, and cultural differences between provinces, it could be important for each province and territory to hold its own vote to ensure that all regions have a say in the decision. A national referendum would set the stage, but the outcome would likely hinge on regional participation and varying levels of support across the country.

For example, provinces with strong historical, economic, and political ties to the U.S., such as Alberta and British Columbia, might be more inclined to support union. In contrast, provinces with a strong sense of Canadian nationalism or those with significant linguistic or cultural differences, such as Quebec, might approach the referendum with more caution, potentially leading to regional divides in the vote.

Implications of a Referendum for Canadian Democracy and Sovereignty

A referendum on whether Canada should become part of the United States would be a critical test of the strength and viability of Canadian democracy and sovereignty. Canada has prided itself on being an independent and sovereign nation since its confederation in 1867, and the question of whether to merge with the U.S. would touch on deeply held principles about national identity, governance, and autonomy.

Democratic Process and Citizen Engagement

One of the fundamental implications of holding a referendum would be its emphasis on direct democracy. In representative democracies, citizens delegate decision making power to elected officials, but a referendum represents an opportunity for the people themselves to directly participate in the shaping of their country's future. The referendum would be a unique moment in Canadian history, where the nation would have the chance to engage in an open debate about its national direction. If handled with transparency and inclusivity, the referendum could deepen citizens' connection to the political process and provide a platform for national conversations about identity, governance, and policy.

However, the referendum process could also raise questions about the effectiveness of such a drastic change being decided by popular vote. Many experts and political leaders might argue that an issue as fundamental as the nation's future should not be determined solely by the whims of the electorate but should instead involve comprehensive deliberation and institutional checks and balances. The sheer gravity of the decision altering Canada's constitutional structure, its political identity, and its place in the world could make it difficult for many to accept the result of a simple majority vote, especially if it is perceived as rushed or uninformed.

Sovereignty and National Independence

At its core, the referendum would be a test of Canada's sovereignty. The notion of becoming part of the United States would entail a massive cession of sovereignty. Canada would no longer control its foreign policy, military, or economic destiny independently. While the U.S. and Canada already have deeply intertwined economic and political systems, formal union would fundamentally change the nature of Canadian sovereignty. Some Canadians might view this as a relinquishment of their nationhood, while others may see it as an opportunity to solidify economic prosperity and strengthen security under the umbrella of a larger power.

The referendum would likely force Canadians to reflect on what it means to be a sovereign nation. What aspects of Canadian life and culture are non-negotiable, and what can be shared or integrated with another country? The tension between maintaining Canada's independent identity and embracing the opportunities presented by union with the U.S. would dominate the referendum debate. For many, the idea of losing control over crucial national decisions, such as foreign policy, military engagements, and immigration laws, would be seen as an unacceptable erosion of Canada's hard-won sovereignty.

Potential Impact on Canadian National Unity

National unity would be one of the most sensitive and divisive issues in a referendum on joining the United States. Canada is a country with a history of regional differences and cultural tensions. The referendum could exacerbate divisions between provinces, territories, and cultural groups, potentially threatening the unity of the nation in ways that go far beyond the question of statehood.

Regional Divides

Canada's regionalism has long been a defining feature of its political landscape. The west, particularly provinces like Alberta, has often felt at odds with the central government in Ottawa, especially over issues like energy policy and fiscal transfers. As a result, these provinces might be more receptive to the idea of joining the U.S., seeing it as a way to increase their political and economic influence. Conversely, regions with more distinct identities such as Quebec, which has long sought greater autonomy or independence from Canada, might see union with the U.S. as an unacceptable loss of national identity.

Polarization and Identity Crisis

The referendum could also provoke a broader identity crisis among Canadians. The decision to join the U.S. would force people to confront the question of what it means to be Canadian. Would Canadian national identity be subsumed into American culture, or would it continue to flourish as part of a larger union? For many Canadians, the question of national identity is intrinsically tied to their sense of pride in being distinct from the U.S. in terms of healthcare, social programs, language, and cultural values.

A divisive referendum could lead to further polarization and fracturing of national unity, especially if the vote were close. If one region or province strongly rejected union while others supported it, the result could deepen divisions that already exist, potentially even threatening the very fabric of Canadian federalism. The issue of Quebec's unique status within Canada, for example, would likely become a central and contentious issue in the referendum.

National Reconciliation

At the same time, the referendum process could create an opportunity for national reconciliation and renewed discussions about Canada's future. Regardless of the outcome, the referendum could spark a nationwide debate about Canadian values, identity, and how the country should move forward in a changing world. For some, the process of debating and deliberating the question could help unite people across regional, linguistic, and political lines in ways that would strengthen Canadian democracy in the long run.

A Moment of Reckoning for Canada

The referendum on whether Canada should become the 51st state would be a defining moment in the country's history. The process would not only determine Canada's future relationship with the United States but also challenge the very foundations of Canadian democracy, sovereignty, and national unity. As Canadians debate the merits and risks of such a monumental change, the referendum would force the nation to reflect deeply on what it means to be Canadian and whether the potential benefits of union with the U.S. outweigh the costs of losing independence and national identity.

The outcome of the referendum could have profound and lasting consequences, reshaping Canadian society and politics, and potentially altering the course of North American history. Whether or not Canada ultimately becomes the 51st state, the process of engaging with this question would provide an opportunity for Canadians to rethink their future in the global community and to confront the challenges and opportunities of a rapidly changing world.

Chapter 21
The Role of the Canadian Government

The prospect of Canada becoming the 51st state of the United States would trigger profound changes in the governance of both nations. The roles and responsibilities of the Canadian and American governments in facilitating the union would be far-reaching, as they would have to navigate a host of legal, political, and institutional challenges. This chapter examines how both governments would play a role in the process of union, the responsibilities and challenges they would face, and the potential implications for their political systems.

The Role of the Canadian and American Governments in the Process of Union

For Canada to become the 51st state, both the Canadian and American governments would be required to engage in complex negotiations and legal processes that would reshape both nations. These discussions would include constitutional changes, the integration of institutions, and the reorganization of political structures.

Canadian Government: A National Decision

The Canadian government, led by the federal government in Ottawa and the provincial governments across the country, would be central to the process of union. Canada's federal system, with its division of powers between provincial and federal governments, would present significant challenges. The Canadian government would need to spearhead the process of dissolving the country's existing political framework and integrating its provinces and territories into the U.S. system.

The first step for Canada's government would likely be to hold a national referendum, as discussed in Chapter 20, to gauge public opinion and secure the support of the Canadian people. This would be a critical test of Canada's democratic principles and would serve as the foundation for the next steps. Once the decision was made to pursue union, the federal government would negotiate the terms with the U.S.

government, which would include economic integration, political representation, and the transfer of sovereignty. The Canadian government would need to work with provincial premiers and territories to ensure that their interests were represented in the union process, particularly concerning the preservation of local cultures, languages, and laws.

A major challenge for the Canadian government would be dealing with regional resistance. Provinces such as Quebec, with its unique linguistic and cultural identity, would need to be carefully engaged in the process to avoid divisions that could potentially fracture the country further. Additionally, the provinces would have to work with the U.S. government to determine how political representation in the U.S. Congress and the Electoral College would be structured for the new states.

American Government: Welcoming a New Member
On the American side, the federal government, led by the President and Congress, would play a pivotal role in admitting Canada as the 51st state. The U.S. Constitution provides a framework for the admission of new states, but the process is highly discretionary and requires both political and constitutional adjustments.

First, Congress would need to pass legislation to admit Canada as a state. This would involve drafting and passing an "Admission Act" that outlines the terms of union, including the specific boundaries of Canada's new states and the logistics of integrating Canada's population into the U.S. The act would also address practical concerns such as the division of economic resources, the integration of Canadian laws and systems, and the creation of a new political structure.

The U.S. government would need to engage with the Canadian government in extensive negotiations to ensure that the terms of the union were agreeable to both parties. This could include discussions about the division of military responsibilities, trade policies, healthcare integration, and the future of Canadian social programs, which would have to be adjusted to fit within the American system.

In terms of political integration, the U.S. government could have to make significant changes to accommodate Canada's population. This would likely involve the creation of new congressional districts to represent the new states, with consideration given to regional and population differences. Additionally, Canada's diverse legal and educational systems would need to be harmonized with American institutions, a process that would require careful planning and cooperation.

Potential Responsibilities and Challenges for Governments

The process of integrating Canada into the United States would require both governments to shoulder immense responsibilities and confront numerous challenges. These responsibilities would range from legal adjustments to social integration, and both governments would need to coordinate to ensure a smooth transition.

For the Canadian Government: Sovereignty and Transition

Canada's government would face the difficult task of transitioning from a sovereign nation to a state within a larger union. The dissolution of Canada's constitutional framework would require extensive constitutional reforms, particularly as Canada's provinces would need to give up their provincial powers in exchange for the rights and responsibilities of U.S. states.

One major challenge would be managing the potential loss of national sovereignty. Canada would no longer be able to control its foreign policy, military, or international relations independently. While this might be seen as beneficial for security reasons given the potential for closer cooperation with the U.S. military, it would be a difficult adjustment for Canadians who are fiercely protective of their autonomy. The

Canadian government would also need to ensure that the rights of minorities, especially French speaking Canadians in Quebec, were safeguarded. The potential loss of Canadian identity and culture would likely become a focal point of debate.

Additionally, the Canadian government would be responsible for managing the integration of Canada's political, economic, and legal systems into the U.S. system. This includes aligning Canada's laws with U.S. federal and state law, transitioning the Canadian dollar to the U.S. dollar, and ensuring that the Canadian healthcare system would mesh with U.S. policies on public health.

For the American Government: Integration and Expansion

The U.S. government would face its own set of challenges in integrating Canada into its political, economic, and social systems. One of the key responsibilities would be ensuring that the new states from Canada were granted fair representation in Congress, which would involve restructuring the U.S. political system. This would mean the creation of new congressional districts, electoral college votes, and potentially new positions in the executive branch.

The U.S. government would also need to help manage the economic transition. Canada's economy would need to be fully integrated into the U.S. economic system, including trade policies, currency transition, and regulatory systems. Although Canada and the U.S. already have strong economic ties, the full integration of Canada's economy into the U.S. system would present both opportunities and challenges. The U.S. government would need to develop policies to address potential economic disruptions, such as fluctuations in labor markets, taxation systems, and trade agreements with other countries.

Social integration would also be a challenge. Canada has a distinct social system, especially regarding healthcare, education, and social welfare programs. The U.S. would need to adjust its systems to accommodate the influx of Canadian citizens, many of whom may have different expectations and experiences with public services. Furthermore, the U.S. government would need to navigate the complex issue of preserving Canadian cultural identities, particularly the French speaking population in Quebec, while blending these diverse communities into the broader American social fabric.

Potential Implications for Canadian and American Politics and Governance

The union of Canada and the United States would have profound implications for both political systems. The integration of a new nation with distinct political and cultural values would alter the dynamics of governance in both countries.

Impact on Canadian Politics

For Canada, becoming a U.S. state would fundamentally change its political system. The dissolution of its parliamentary system would shift governance to the American system of federalism. Canadians would no longer elect Members of Parliament (MPs) to a federal Parliament in Ottawa but would instead vote for representatives in the U.S. Congress. This would dramatically change the political landscape, as provinces that previously had significant political power in Canada's system would now be reduced to state level influence within the U.S.

The shift would certainly disrupt Canadian political parties, which have evolved to reflect the specific needs and priorities of Canadian society. New political parties could emerge within the U.S. to represent the interests of Canadian states, and Canadian political ideologies might be reoriented to fit into the broader context of American politics. For example, parties such as the Bloc Québécois, which advocates for the interests of French speaking Canadians, would likely dissolve or rebrand themselves to advocate for Quebec's place within the U.S.

Impact on American Politics

The American political system would also experience a dramatic transformation. The addition of new states would not only alter the balance of power in Congress but also shift the electoral dynamics of presidential elections. The addition of millions of new citizens would likely have a significant impact on party politics, with both Democrats and Republicans vying for the support of Canadian voters who may bring new political priorities and perspectives into the U.S. political debate.

Moreover, the integration of Canadian governance into the U.S. system would require an adaptation to a federal model that would have to account for the unique characteristics of Canada's political history and institutions. The question of whether the U.S. political parties would successfully incorporate Canadian political structures into their own platforms would be a key challenge.

Foreign Policy and Governance

Finally, the union would shift both countries' foreign policy dynamics. Canada's historical ties to Britain and the Commonwealth, as well as its role as a middle power in international diplomacy, would have to be reconciled with U.S. foreign policy. The U.S. government would assume full responsibility for Canadian international relations, potentially altering the country's role in the United Nations, NATO, and other international bodies. This could lead to shifts in U.S. policy toward global issues such as climate change, trade agreements, and military interventions, as Canadian priorities would now be incorporated into the broader American foreign policy agenda.

A Momentous Challenge for Both Governments

The process of Canada becoming the 51st state would require significant coordination between the Canadian and American governments. Both would need to address legal, political, economic, and social challenges as they navigate this complex union. While there would be substantial benefits in terms of economic integration, security, and political influence, the challenges of preserving cultural identity, managing regional differences, and restructuring governance systems would be formidable.

Ultimately, the process of union would not only transform the two countries' political landscapes but would also redefine their roles in the global order. It would be a process of negotiation, adaptation, and, at times, compromise, requiring the cooperation of governments on both sides of the border to ensure a smooth transition. The roles of the Canadian and American governments would be central to this transformation, as they would guide their countries through the difficult terrain of unification and help shape the future of North America.

Chapter 22
The Future of Canada-US Relations

If Canada were to become the 51st state of the United States, the longstanding relationship between the two countries would be fundamentally transformed. What has traditionally been a close, yet separate relationship between two sovereign nations would evolve into a new political and economic integration under a single federal system. This chapter will explore the potential future of Canada U.S. relations in such a scenario, considering the opportunities and challenges that would arise from this profound shift. We will also discuss how this transformation could impact broader North American integration and cooperation.

The Potential Future of Canada-U.S. Relations if Canada Becomes the 51st State

Historically, Canada and the U.S. have shared an extraordinarily close relationship characterized by deep economic ties, shared values, and significant cultural interaction. The two countries are the largest trading partners in the world, with highly integrated economies, interconnected infrastructure, and mutual interests in security and global governance. However, despite these ties, each nation has remained politically distinct, with separate identities, legal frameworks, and international alliances.

If Canada were to join the United States as the 51st state, this close relationship would shift from one of neighbors and allies to that of a single political entity. Canada's integration into the U.S. would mean that many of the shared policies and interests would be formalized into a new and comprehensive union. This would likely lead to a more seamless economic relationship, a unified foreign policy, and deeper political coordination. However, the transformation would not be without complexities, as the integration of a nation with its own distinct political and cultural identity into the U.S. system would present challenges on several fronts.

Political Integration

One of the most profound changes would be the integration of Canadian governance into the U.S. federal system. Provinces like Ontario, British Columbia, and Quebec would become part of the new 51st U.S. state, represented in Congress and the Electoral College. This would significantly shift the balance of political power in the U.S., as Canada's population of over 38 million would add substantial representation to both houses of Congress. The political dynamics of the United States would therefore evolve, as the Canadian electorate would bring new priorities and concerns into the national political debate.

Cultural and Identity Integration

Canada's unique cultural identity, shaped by its bilingualism, Indigenous communities, and its historical ties to Britain, would be integrated into the broader American cultural fabric. While the U.S. is often seen as a "melting pot," where diverse cultural backgrounds are blended into a cohesive national identity, the Canadian cultural mosaic emphasizing multiculturalism and bilingualism would offer a new dynamic. The integration of Canada's linguistic and cultural diversity into the U.S. system would require adjustments on both sides, as Americans could need to reconcile their identity as a superpower with the potential inclusion of

Canadian values, such as social welfare programs and a commitment to peacekeeping and diplomacy.

Potential Opportunities and Challenges for the Relationship

The integration of Canada into the U.S. would present both substantial opportunities and significant challenges. While the prospect of greater cooperation, economic integration, and political cohesion could benefit both countries, the changes involved would also raise important questions about national identity, governance, and the future direction of the North American continent.

Opportunities for Strengthening Economic Ties

Canada's integration into the U.S. would likely result in the complete integration of the two countries' economies, which are already highly interconnected. The U.S. Canada trade relationship, worth over $1 trillion annually, would expand even further. Canada's resources, particularly in oil, natural gas, and minerals could be more easily distributed throughout the U.S. economy, creating new economic opportunities for both nations. The combined economic power of a unified North American market would also allow for greater influence on the global stage, particularly in the context of trade negotiations, especially with other large economic powers like China and the European Union.

The harmonization of regulations, currencies, and tax systems would also be a major benefit. The Canadian dollar would become the U.S. dollar, and Canadian businesses would be able to operate more seamlessly within the American market without the need for cross border regulations or tariffs. This would likely lower transaction costs and promote further economic cooperation in areas such as infrastructure, technology, and energy.

Political and Social Cooperation

As a new state within the U.S., Canada would bring with it a commitment to progressive social policies such as universal healthcare and an emphasis on human rights and environmental protections. These values could influence American governance and may lead to broader discussions about how the U.S. can incorporate some of Canada's more socially progressive policies into its own system.

At the same time, Canada's existing systems of social welfare, healthcare, and environmental protections would need to be integrated into U.S. systems. The U.S. government would face the challenge of reconciling differing approaches to social policies, such as healthcare, which might require a significant overhaul of the American system to align with Canadian practices. While many Canadians have long admired the American political system, some may feel that certain aspects of their own country's social policies could be threatened by the shift.

Cultural Exchange and Unity

Culturally, Canada's integration into the U.S. would bring new perspectives on immigration, diversity, and multiculturalism. Canadians, who place a high value on inclusivity and bilingualism, would likely advocate for policies that embrace cultural diversity in American society. The greater representation of French speaking Canadians, particularly from Quebec, would further enrich the diversity of the U.S., adding to the already complex tapestry of American identity.

However, integrating Canada's unique culture could also present challenges. The distinct Canadian identity, which has evolved over centuries, might face erosion within the broader American political system. Canadians may struggle with the loss of their independent political structures, international voice, and national symbols. For instance, Canada's strong tradition of peacekeeping and neutrality in global conflicts might conflict with U.S. policies and military interventions, raising questions about how Canadian identity could be preserved within the larger American framework.

Regional Tensions and Political Representation

One major challenge would be ensuring that Canada's diverse regional interests are respected within the U.S. system. Canada's provinces, such as Quebec, which has a large French speaking population, have often demanded, and gotten special treatment and recognition within Canada's federal system. The integration of Quebec and other provinces into the U.S. system could lead to tensions around the issue of political representation and the desire for continued cultural autonomy.

The addition of a large number of new states would also shift the power dynamics within the U.S. government, potentially leading to political friction. The inclusion of a Canadian state, particularly in the Senate, could lead to an imbalance in political power, with some states feeling that their interests are sidelined by the larger Canadian region. This could create new political divides and calls for regional representation or greater devolution of power, as the American system might struggle to accommodate Canada's diverse cultural and political landscape.

Potential Implications for North American Integration and Cooperation

If Canada were to become the 51st state, the broader question of North American integration would evolve in significant ways. The concept of a united North America, economically, politically, and socially would take on a new dimension, as the U.S., Canada, and Mexico may be more tightly bound within the framework of a single, integrated political entity.

Deeper Economic Integration

The creation of a unified North American market could bring Canada, the U.S., and Mexico into an even closer economic relationship. While the North American Free Trade Agreement (NAFTA) has already encouraged free trade and economic cooperation between these nations, the integration of Canada into the U.S. would likely streamline economic transactions across the continent. The free flow of goods, services, and labor would create new opportunities for North American businesses, especially in industries like energy, technology, and manufacturing.

A unified North American economy could also offer greater leverage in global trade negotiations. As a single entity, North America would be able to negotiate with other global powers, such as China and the European Union, from a position of greater strength. A harmonized trade policy and coordinated economic strategy would reduce barriers to entry and increase global competitiveness.

Security and Environmental Cooperation

The integration of Canada into the U.S. would also deepen security cooperation across North America. The shared defense arrangements between Canada and the U.S. would be formalized, allowing for a more unified approach to defense and military strategy. The North American Aerospace Defense Command (NORAD) could become a more centralized institution, with both nations working together to protect their joint borders, combat terrorism, and manage security challenges in the Western Hemisphere.

Environmental cooperation would likely increase as well, with shared concerns about climate change, resource management, and conservation. Canada's vast natural resources such as its forests, oil sands, and water systems would be more easily managed in tandem with U.S. policy, potentially leading to greater environmental protections and joint initiatives to combat ecological threats.

Political Challenges and National Identity

While deeper integration would undoubtedly offer economic and security benefits, the political and social challenges could be significant. The question of national identity would remain one of the most sensitive issues. Canada's distinct cultural and political history would not be easily erased, and the integration of this history into the broader U.S. narrative would require considerable effort. Tensions around language, diversity, and regional autonomy would likely arise as Canadians navigated their new role as U.S. citizens.

A New Era of North American Unity and Complexity

The future of Canada-U.S. relations in the event of Canada becoming the 51st state would be a complex but promising chapter in the history of North America. While this transformation would present significant opportunities for economic integration, political cooperation, and regional stability, it would also come with its own set of challenges. The integration of Canadian culture, political systems, and governance into the U.S. framework would require careful balancing, while issues of regional representation, identity, and autonomy would continue to be hotly debated.

Ultimately, Canada's entry into the U.S. as the 51st state could represent a next step in North American cooperation. It may create new opportunities for collective growth and influence on the global stage, while also necessitating ongoing dialogue to ensure the diverse needs of both countries are met.

Chapter 23

Hypothetical Statistics, Charts and Comparisons to Other Countries and Continents, Post Union

If Canada were to become the 51st state of the United States, it would significantly alter the demographic, economic, political, and geopolitical landscape. To help understand these changes, let's compare the newly unified U.S. now including Canada, with other countries and continents across various key metrics, such as population, land size, GDP, and other factors. This will provide a sense of scale and context for what the U.S. with Canada as a state would look like compared to the rest of the world.

Population	• **Total Population**:
	  ○ **USA (current)**: 332 million
	  ○ **Canada (current)**: 39 million
	USA + Canada (Post-Union):
	• **Population**: 371 million
	Population Comparison with Other Countries
	• **China**: 1.43 billion (4.4x the combined U.S. and Canada population)
	• **India**: 1.42 billion (4.3x the combined U.S. and Canada population)
	• **European Union**: 447 million (1.2x the combined U.S. and Canada population)
	• **Brazil**: 213 million (0.57x the combined U.S. and Canada population)
	Mexico: 134 million (0.36x the combined U.S. and Canada population)

Land Size	○ **USA (current)**: 9.8 million square kilometers (3.78 million square miles) ○ **Canada (current)**: 9.98 million square kilometers (3.85 million square miles) **USA + Canada (Post-Union)**: **Land Size**: 19.78 million square kilometers (7.64 million square miles) **Comparisons with Other Countries**:

	• **Russia**: 17.1 million square kilometers (6.60 million square miles) *still larger than the combined U.S. + Canada • **China**: 9.6 million square kilometers (3.71 million square miles) *half the size of the combined U.S. and Canada • **Brazil**: 8.5 million square kilometers (3.28 million square miles) *smaller than the combined U.S. and Canada by about half • **Australia**: 7.7 million square kilometers (2.97 million square miles) *about 39% the size of the combined U.S. and Canada **Comparison with Continents**: • **Africa**: 30.37 million square kilometers (11.73 million square miles) *1.5x the size of the combined U.S. and Canada • **Asia**: 44.58 million square kilometers (17.21 million square miles) *2.26x the size of the combined U.S. and Canada • **Europe**: 10.18 million square kilometers (3.93 million square miles) *slightly larger than the U.S. + Canada by about 3%
GDP Post Union	**USA + Canada (Post-Union)**: • **GDP**: $28.2 trillion ($26 trillion from the U.S. + $2.2 trillion from Canada) **Comparisons with Other Countries**: • **China**: $17.7 trillion *lower GDP than the combined U.S. + Canada, but still a significant global economic power

	• **India**: $3.7 trillion *far smaller than the combined U.S. + Canada GDP • **Japan**: $4.9 trillion *smaller than the combined U.S. + Canada by more than half • **Germany**: $5.3 trillion *also smaller by more than half compared to the combined GDP • **United Kingdom**: $3.2 trillion *less than 12% of the combined GDP of the U.S. and Canada
Political Influence (United Nations & Global Organizations)	**Post-Union U.S.:** • **UN Security Council**: The U.S. already holds a permanent seat, and the addition of Canada would further consolidate its influence within the Security Council, as Canada has historically been a strong advocate for multilateralism and diplomacy. **Comparison with Other Countries**: • **China and Russia**: Both have veto power in the UN Security Council. The post-union U.S. would strengthen its position as the dominant Western global power. • **European Union**: While the EU is a powerful economic and political bloc, it does not have a single unified voice in global governance comparable to a superpower like the U.S. + Canada combined.

Demographics	• **Age Distribution**:
	   ○ **Median Age of USA**: 38 years
	   ○ **Median Age of Canada**: 41 years
	   ○ Combine for a median age of

	39.3 years.
Urban vs Rural	o **Urban Population in USA**: 82% o **Urban Population in Canada**: 81% o After union, **82% of 371 million = 304 million urban, 68 million rural**.
Languages and Cultural Diversity Comparison	**USA + Canada (Post-Union)**: **Languages**: • **English**: 70% (Approximately 260 million people) • **French**: 20% (Approximately 74 million people) • **Other languages**: 10% (Approximately 37 million people) o The addition of French speaking Canadians primarily in Quebec would make the post-union U.S. one of the largest bilingual countries in the world. **Comparison with Other Countries**: • **India**: Hindi and English are official, but with 22 languages recognized in the constitution, India is arguably the most linguistically diverse country in the world. • **Switzerland**: Four official languages (German, French, Italian, and Romansh), and a highly multilingual society. • **European Union**: 24 official languages, with multiple linguistic minorities and regional languages.
Economic Strength & Weakness GDP	**USA + Canada (Post-Union)**: o **USA (current)**: $26 trillion

	<ul><li>**Canada (current)**: \$2.2 trillion</li><li>**Total GDP**: \$28.2 trillion</li></ul>**Comparisons with Other Countries**:<ul><li>**China**: \$17.7 trillion (lower GDP than the combined U.S. + Canada, but still a significant global economic power)</li><li>**India**: \$3.7 trillion (far smaller than the combined U.S. + Canada GDP)</li><li>**Japan**: \$4.9 trillion (smaller than the combined U.S. + Canada by more than half)</li><li>**Germany**: \$5.3 trillion (also smaller by more than half compared to the combined GDP)</li><li>**United Kingdom**: \$3.2 trillion (less than 12% of the combined GDP of the U.S. and Canada)</li></ul>**Comparison with Continents**:<ul><li>**Asia**: \$33.7 trillion (larger than the combined U.S. and Canada GDP)</li><li>**Europe**: \$23.5 trillion (still smaller than the combined GDP of the U.S. and Canada, but approaching it)</li><li>**Africa**: \$3.6 trillion (roughly 13% the size of the combined U.S. and Canada GDP)</li></ul>
Main Industries	<ul><li>**USA**: Technology, Finance, Healthcare, Manufacturing</li><li>**Canada**: Energy (oil, natural gas), Timber, Mining, Aerospace</li></ul>
Economic Weaknesses	<ul><li>**USA**: Income inequality, Healthcare system cost</li><li>**Canada**: Dependency on resource exports, Regional economic disparities</li></ul>

Religious Composition	**USA + Canada (Post-Union):** • **Christianity**: 70% • **Non-religious**: 25% • **Other religions (Hinduism, Islam, Judaism, etc.)**: 5% **Comparison with Other Countries:** • **India**: Predominantly Hindu (79%), with significant Muslim (14%) and Christian minorities. • **Saudi Arabia**: Nearly 100% Muslim. • **Israel**: Predominantly Jewish (74%), with Muslim and Christian minorities. • **Brazil**: Mostly Christian (87%), with smaller percentages of other religions.

Political Structure	• **States and Provinces:**
	   o **USA (current):** 50 states
	   o **Canada:** 10 provinces, 3 territories
	   o Post-union: **51 states or 63 states if each province and territory is separately included**

Military Strength Comparison	**USA + Canada (Post-Union):** • **United States**: $750 billion (still the largest defense budget in the world) • **Canada**: $41 billion • **Total Military Budget**: Approximately close to $800 billion (combined defense spending of the U.S. and Canada) **Comparisons with Other Countries:** • **China**: $261 billion (far smaller than the combined U.S. + Canada budget)

	• **Russia**: $65 billion (about 8% of the combined U.S. and Canada defense budget) • **India**: $73 billion (roughly 9% of the combined U.S. and Canada defense budget) • **European Union**: $313 billion (a little less than half of the combined U.S. + Canada defense budget)
Environmental Impact	**USA + Canada (Post-Union)**: • **Carbon Emissions**: With Canada's substantial reliance on oil and gas exports and the U.S.'s high per capita emissions, the combined U.S. and Canada would be one of the largest emitters of greenhouse gases in the world. **Comparison with Other Countries**: • **China**: Currently the world's largest emitter, with about 28% of global emissions. • **India**: The third-largest emitter, though still far below the U.S. and China. • **European Union**: Combined emissions of EU countries are significant but lower than the U.S. + Canada. • **Russia**: High per capita emissions, but overall emissions are lower than the combined U.S. and Canada.

In conclusion, the U.S. with Canada as the 51st State would have a profound impact on global power dynamics. The union would result in the world's second-largest population and a nearly 20 million square kilometer land area, making it the largest combined country by land size, and the largest economic entity by GDP. It would have significant geopolitical, military, and cultural influence, continuing to play a dominant role in global affairs, trade, and security.

The hypothetical scenario of Canada becoming the 51st state of the United States opens up a wide array of considerations about governance, economics, culture, and identity. While the prospect of such a union may be far-fetched, it provides a valuable thought experiment that challenges our assumptions about national boundaries, political systems, and the evolving nature of international relations.

As the world continues to grow more interconnected, the relationships between neighboring nations will remain vital. Whether or not Canada ever becomes the 51st state, the importance of Canada-U.S. relations and the future of North American cooperation will continue to shape the political and economic landscape for generations to come.

Chapter 24
A New Era for North America
Food for thought!

The hypothetical scenario of Canada becoming the 51st state of the United States is a profound and thought-provoking concept that raises a multitude of questions, economic, political, cultural, and historical. Throughout this book, we have explored various facets of what such a monumental shift would mean for both Canada and the United States. From the intricate dynamics of trade and economics to the challenges of political integration, we have touched on the opportunities and obstacles that would accompany such a union. In this concluding chapter, we will reflect on the broader implications of Canada's potential statehood and the future of North America in a rapidly changing world.

The Complex Reality of Union

While the idea of Canada becoming the 51st state is intriguing, it remains largely a speculative notion. The relationship between Canada and the United States, though deeply interconnected, is one that has been shaped by centuries of shared history and distinct political, social, and cultural identities. The possibility of Canada shedding its sovereignty and merging with the U.S. represents an extreme shift, one that challenges fundamental assumptions about national identity, governance, and international relations.

If such a union were ever to occur, the process would undoubtedly be complex and fraught with challenges. The integration of Canada into the U.S. would require not only the adjustment of policies, legal frameworks, and institutions but also a deep transformation in the way Canadians and Americans view their shared history and collective future. The political process of achieving this union, from referendum to ratification, would likely take years, if not decades, and would require immense political will and support on both sides of the border.

Economic and Political Implications

The economic implications of Canada joining the U.S. would be far reaching. The seamless integration of the two countries' economies could bring unprecedented benefits such as trade barriers would be eliminated, markets would become more integrated, and industries such as energy, technology, and agriculture could experience growth on a massive scale. With Canada's vast natural resources, such as oil, timber, and minerals, and its highly skilled workforce, the U.S. could secure even more economic dominance in global markets.

However, these economic advantages would come at a price. The integration of a large and diverse country like Canada into the U.S. would shift the balance of political power. Canada's distinct political, social, and environmental policies would need to be reconciled with those of the U.S., potentially creating friction on issues such as healthcare, social welfare, and environmental regulation. The U.S. political system, already polarized, would face further challenges as Canada's provinces and their unique needs sought representation and recognition in Washington.

Cultural and National Identity

One of the most profound impacts of Canada becoming the 51st state would be on cultural identity. For Canadians, the loss of sovereignty would represent the end of an era of independent nationhood, with all the cultural and symbolic significance that comes with it. Canada's rich history, its French English bilingual heritage, its commitment to multiculturalism, and its distinct social policies would all be altered in the context of American governance.

The U.S. itself would also experience shifts in its cultural and political identity, as Canada's inclusion would introduce new dynamics into American society. Canadian values such as inclusivity, bilingualism, and a strong commitment to social welfare would reshape American political discourse and social policies. However, the challenge would lie in maintaining a coherent national identity in a vast and diverse country and ensuring that Canadian values would be incorporated without undermining American traditions and ideals.

Moreover, the integration of Quebec and its Francophone population would present a unique challenge. Quebec's history, language, and culture are deeply intertwined with its identity as a distinct political entity. Incorporating Quebec into the American system would require careful negotiation to maintain its cultural autonomy while also blending it into the broader American fabric.

Implications for North American Cooperation

If Canada were to become the 51st state, it would lead to a dramatic shift in the political landscape of North America. The existing NAFTA framework would possibly need to evolve into a unified North American economic zone, consolidating resources, trade agreements, and infrastructure. The U.S. and Canada would be united under one political system, making it easier to tackle regional issues such as climate change, immigration, and border security.

This closer cooperation could provide an opportunity for North America to become a more integrated and influential geopolitical force in the world. As one of the largest and most resource-rich regions on the planet, a unified North American bloc could leverage its economic power to influence global trade, technology, and environmental policies.

Yet, this unity could also face challenges, as the political systems of two distinct countries, each with its own history, culture, and values would have to be reconciled. The governance of such a diverse region would require a level of cooperation and compromise that might be difficult to achieve, especially given the tensions that have historically existed between the U.S. and Canada on issues such as trade and environmental protection.

The Future of Canada-U.S. Relations

While the idea of Canada becoming the 51st state remains speculative, it serves as a lens through which we can explore the potential for deeper cooperation between the U.S. and Canada. The relationship between the two countries is already strong, with deep economic, political, and cultural ties. Trade between the U.S. and Canada is vital to both nations, and their security cooperation through institutions like NORAD has been critical for maintaining regional stability.

If Canada were to become part of the U.S., it would represent the culmination of a long history of bilateral cooperation, but it would also introduce a host of new complexities. The integration of Canadian governance, culture, and policies into the American system would require not just political will but also a shared vision for the future of North America. For many Canadians, the idea of losing sovereignty and becoming a part of the U.S. would be unappealing, while others might see the potential for increased prosperity and security. Ultimately, the future of Canada-U.S. relations depends not just on the economic and political factors but on the cultural and historical ties that bind the two nations together.

The Unlikely but Thought-Provoking Possibility

In the end, the notion of Canada becoming the 51st state remains an unlikely one. Despite the many opportunities such a union could present like economic integration, greater political influence, and a more united North America, the complexities and challenges are vast. The differences in political culture, national identity, and governance systems between Canada and the U.S. are deeply entrenched, and it is difficult to imagine a smooth process of integration. Furthermore, the fundamental idea of national sovereignty remains one of the cornerstones of both Canadian and American identities, making it a difficult concept for many to accept.

Yet, the mere possibility of such a union prompts important questions about the future of North American cooperation. It forces us to consider how two powerful neighbors, with shared interests and challenges, can continue to evolve together in a rapidly changing world. The relationship between Canada and the U.S. is likely to remain one of the most important in global geopolitics, regardless of the form it takes.

REFERENCES

Canadian Constitution: Constitution Act, 1867.

American Constitution: United States Constitution, 1787.

Canadian Charter of Rights and Freedoms: Canadian Charter of Rights and Freedoms, 1982.

American Bill of Rights: United States Bill of Rights, 1791.

"The Canadian Constitution" by Peter W. Hogg.

"The American Constitution" by Akhil Reed Amar.

"The Canadian Charter of Rights and Freedoms" by Robert J. Sharpe.

"The American Bill of Rights" by Bernard Schwartz.

Appendices

1. **Appendix A**: Canadian Constitution.

2. **Appendix B**: American Constitution.

3. **Appendix C**: Canadian Charter of Rights and Freedoms.

4. **Appendix D**: American Bill of Rights.

Royal Commission on Aboriginal Peoples. (1996). Report of the Royal Commission on Aboriginal Peoples.

Indian Act, R.S.C. 1985, c. I-5.

Truth and Reconciliation Commission of Canada. (2015). Honouring the Truth, Reconciling for the Future: Summary of the Final Report of the Truth and Reconciliation Commission of Canada.

Inquiry into Missing and Murdered Indigenous Women and Girls. (2019). Reclaiming Power and Place: The Final Report of the National Inquiry into Missing and Murdered Indigenous Women and Girls.

Carney, R. (2019). Why Canada should become the 51st state. The Globe and Mail.

McMartin, P. (2019). Why the U.S. should be Canada's 11th province. The Vancouver Sun.

Treaty of Niagara, 1764.

Indian Reorganization Act, 25 U.S.C. § 461 et seq.

Official Languages Act, R.S.C. 1985, c. 31.

Canadian Multiculturalism Act, R.S.C. 1985, c. 24.

Sechelt Indian Band Self-Government Act, S.C. 1988, c. 27.

Historical Resources

War Plan Red (1930s) - A declassified U.S. military plan outlining strategies for invading Canada in the event of a conflict with the British Empire. Accessible through the U.S. National Archives.

The Annexation Manifesto (1849) - A historical document from Canadian merchants and politicians advocating for union with the United States.

19th-Century Annexation Debates - Parliamentary records and editorials discussing the political movements supporting annexation in the late 1800s.

Legal and Treaty-Based Resources

The U.S. Constitution, Article II, Section 2 - Governs treaty-making powers, which would play a role in any formal annexation process.

North American Free Trade Agreement (NAFTA) and **United States-Mexico-Canada Agreement (USMCA)** - Demonstrate frameworks for economic cooperation and their limitations regarding sovereignty.

The British North America Act (1867) - The foundational document for Canadian confederation, relevant to discussions about sovereignty and external influence.

Opinion-Based Articles and Books

"Why Canada Will Never Become the 51st State" - A 2025 opinion piece published in *Dal News*, analyzing cultural and political barriers.

"The Case for Annexation" - A provocative editorial in *The Atlantic* (2011) exploring hypothetical benefits of unification.

"The 51st State?" by Seymour Martin Lipset - A scholarly analysis of U.S.-Canada relations in the 20th century, discussing economic and cultural integration.

"Why Canadians Will Always Say No" - A critical essay in *The Globe and Mail*, reflecting on national identity and the risks of cultural absorption.

Contemporary Debates

"Trump\u2019s Remarks on Canada: Serious or Sarcastic?" - A 2025 *New York Times* article examining recent comments and public reaction.

Gallup Polls on U.S.-Canada Relations - Surveys reflecting public opinion on cross-border integration over the years.

CBC News Panel Discussions - Ongoing televised debates about the merits and drawbacks of closer integration with the U.S.

Academic Studies

"Economic Implications of Political Integration" - A research paper analyzing how merging economies would impact trade, labor markets, and taxation.

"Cultural Sovereignty vs. Globalization" - A comparative study of Canada and the U.S., focusing on identity in the age of globalization.

Online Archives and Platforms

U.S. National Archives and Records Administration - For historical documents like War Plan Red.

Library and Archives Canada - A comprehensive source of Canadian government records and treaties.

Project Gutenberg - For historical texts and debates on annexation.

www.ingramcontent.com/pod-product-compliance
Lightning Source LLC
Chambersburg PA
CBHW051244020426
42333CB00025B/3039